Published by ScruffyRed Press Ltd
Kilmarnock
www.scruffyred.com

The right of Allan Jackson to be identified as the author of this work, has been asserted by him in accordance with the Copyright, Designs and Patent Act, 1988.
© ScuffyRed.com, 2014

ISBN: 978-1-326-02639-4

All rights reserved. No part of this publication may be reproduced, stored in a retrieval system, or transmitted in any other form or by any other means, electronic, mechanical, photocopying, recording or otherwise without prior permission of the publishers. This book may not be lent, hired out, resold or otherwise disposed of by way of trade in any form of binding or cover other than that in which it is published, without the prior consent of the publishers.

Designed and typeset by ScruffyRed.com
Cover design © alwhite.tumblr.com

To contact the author: -
aricozanical@gmail.com

And So...

When I try to think of all the people, experiences and events that have inspired me over the course of writing Arico Zanical I find the list to be endless. This story has been a close friend of mine for a long time and I hope that in sharing it with the world it can help others in some way. I need to give special thanks to my mother, my brothers, my grandparents, my uncle and his family, my cousins, Ana Wilson and her grammar police, Al White (alwhite.tumblr.com) for his epic Art work, John Grant for having the faith to publish the story, my old friends, the new friends I have made along the way, music, planet earth and all its amazing-ness, the light, the dark, that place in-between and the eternal masterful genius of the cosmos... good luck and enjoy the journey.

Allan

Where the Nomads Roam...

Through a looking glass, to a distant past,
where the nomads laugh is place I find myself
Where the lions roar, where the vultures soar,
where the wild rains pour,
it's a home but there must be more
On the horizon, there's a moon rising,
where Orions arrow points to somewhere new
Gonna take these tools, hunter gather rules,
primitive but true I was born now to explore

And I want to go, when loves not loved here anymore
So I leave to you, bones and stones in a frozen view

As a tribe we choose, as a pride we move,
to survive we prove that we can carry on
In the morning five, in the evening four,
every day death takes away another soul
In the heat we bake, in the cold we shake,
every child we make gonna even up the score
In my dreams I see,
nature shaping we through the family tree,
I will live to it let be

And I want to go, when loves not loved here anymore
So I leave to you, bones and stones in a frozen view

From the foundation, through the formation,
civilisation was just the start
From the sheltered caves, images engraved,
to the lost and saved so close yet far apart
To the future teach, unimagined feats,
promised lands in reach and I can not fail
Through the wind and hale, through the ice and shale,
through the mountain trails I must prevail

And I want to go, when loves not loved here anymore
So I leave to you, bones and stones in a frozen view

...Meets Tumbleweed

Tumbleweed rose up and took the lead,
when the rust ate through the shackles
and the movement was freed
Steel beach and cloud atlas within reach,
simple sermon to the vermin as the vice crusher preach
And did you figure with the trigger you were bigger,
or deeper than the weeper of the mass grave digger?
Blown off course as you diverse from the source,
follow divine signs and bread crumb trails
from a higher force

Vagabonds rest by utopias ponds,
with the swans reflecting elephants where
dreamers wave their magic wands
Inquisitive artistic spirits come to visit,
pass enlightenment to those with the
strength of mind to live it
Wilderness opens gateways full of bliss,
building dynasties around the power
of the geishas kiss
Dragonflies singing the language of disguise,
as the fool change the spool living life
through the cameras eyes

Landscape merge into the view now too escape,
pay the toll, lose control take a journey

through the star gate
Enchantment as you dock at the embankment,
free mind too find your not the puzzle just a fragment
Rendezvous as the love catch up with you,
off the map there is a gap, a greatness that surrounds you
Reflection, living orchestra connection and
when it plays in tune your listening too perfection!

Contents

Zero 11
One 15
Two 21
Three 25
Four 37
Five 43
Six 49
Seven 55
Eight 59
Nine 63
Ten 67
Eleven 77
Twelve 89
Thirteen 107
Fourteen 115
Fifteen 133
Sixteen 143
Seventeen 147
Eighteen 151
Nineteen 167
Twenty 177

Chapter Zero

As I woke up this morning my mind was at rest,
I'd had a sweet dream of a woman undressed.
I looked at the clock it read quarter past eight
"Oh shit not again", for my work I was late.
I kissed the girl by my side and left her to sleep, chucked my uniform on and ran off down the street. As I got to the office my boss he awaits with a red angered face cause I'm a few minutes late. He looked at his watch and his face filled with glee, his expression read 'I own this time, your soul belongs to me'. I think you pay my bills so I'll listen to you, a hierarchical assault what more could I do? He growled "What's your excuse and it had better be good?" testing my obedience like a good master should. I say "I respect you so I'll tell you it true, but you're not gonna like it and I hope you don't sue. I was up all night loving and that was my strife, now here comes the punch line boss this isn't life!"

When I got back to the flat it was empty of life. I made my way to the bathroom and washed the blood from my face. Van Gough would have been proud of the job my now ex-boss had made. I walked through to the bedroom. The bed was neatly made and a note lay on the pillow. It read "It's been fun but I won't be back". Another meaningless relationship was lost in the mist. At least she had made the bed.

I looked at the mail. It was bills for the overdue rent and rented possessions. I was weighed down and sinking. Without being aware of it, I had become dependent on a number of unnecessary material wastes that barely provided satisfaction. I'd been captured in an empty way of life. This I had to change I thought, though when you believe something to be a necessity and are not aware that it's just something you want, it can be very difficult to change. I needed a little help and to be shown another option. I was lost. I needed to find my way.

I went to the kitchen and opened the cupboard door. I was faced with a selection of my favorite medicine bottles, namely a bottle of whisky, some cheap imported vodka, a slice of rum, a dabble of port, some beer and half a bottle of tequila with worm included.

Everything, including the worm, disappeared faster than smoke in the wind. I chain smoked, and began swallowing pill after pill. Some prescribed by doctors, some by dealers. I'd forgotten what the difference was.

Frustration grew consuming me; many little events creating the same feeling were merging, collecting and becoming a mass of its own. Everywhere I looked I saw the same. I shook my head with a hope of unsettling the dust of confusion that had fallen over my eyes with no returns. I was grasping at the air as if drowning in the bubble of similarity surrounding me.

I stumbled and fell to the kitchen floor. I rolled over onto my back and as I looked upwards the lampshade appeared to be moving across the ceiling, like a stingray coasting across a clear ocean floor. A glint of glass from underneath the fridge caught my eye; I reached out and took the object in my right hand. It was a glass compass. The dial was spinning around and would not settle to a single direction. I felt the walls around me were closing in, getting tighter and more strangling with every thought of similarity smashing together more quickly, as the distance between understandings decreased. The storm was brewing. Within the storms eye was the solution. A map was discovered. The map was created through a willingness to find the way. There was nothing less than good intentions... I lashed out at these walls to break a way free, to clear a path in the mist. The movement was echoed by a sound. The smash of the compass was a frightening lightning before my eyes, the sound off the glass breaking against the wall, and against my hand, a fleshy thunder in this exploded blood glass firework.

I looked at my hand for I could focus once more. It was an untidy mortal mess. A portrait of the world I thought. My wrist was open, my mortality apparent and in doubtable. The storm was over, and in the aftermath all was still, all was tranquil. There was no pain.

There was no time for reflection, as the wound had to be healed. Survival instincts grew inside, flowing through my body, and on reaching my feet began to move me to the nearest beacon of aide.

The hospital was a haze of morphine and questions that I had no will or capability to answer. How did it happen? Was it an accident? Were you alone? How do you feel? What have you taken? Are you in pain? Do you have someone you need to contact?

I could only stare into the abyss of what was happening

around me, absorbing the knock on effects of my actions. Soon enough I was in an operating theatre with the kind aliens in white surrounding me, ready to begin fixing nature. The gas kicked in, the darkness came, and there was peace at last.

Chapter One

The dream of feet...

There was no sweat on my brow, though I felt as though I'd been surrounded in a monsoon rain for as long as eternity could bear to last. I was not awake, I was not asleep, I was not moving and I was not standing still. I was in a place where none of that bore any meaning or purpose. There was someone, some thing, some presence or some being next to me, so close, almost inside me, it could even have been me.

A series of situations I'd already thought to have survived through were brought before me, as if I was reliving a distant memory.

The first, was in a darkened bar. There was florescent lights flashing, rolling up and down, hitting a group of darkened silhouettes dancing in colorful organic light. There was no sound and the silhouettes were moving to their own unique rhythm, making movement to their own baseline, to their own call of prayer. Through some telepathic link, the being passed onto me the feeling of wonder and an air of questioning the cause and consequence of the environment I found myself in. Through this telepathic link I suggested to the being, for I don't like to tell, some of them need to keep going, some need to stop, and some just enjoy the movements. The explanation seemed to satisfy, for in a click, as if a quantum leap, we were moved onto, not the next as in a series, more just another situation as out of randomness.

There was a beast of some humanness form wandering around a dimly lit street. There were no others around. The street had no defining characteristics; the buildings lining the pathway were lifeless, hiding in the dark as if to cover their faces. The road itself bore a resemblance to a cobble jigsaw and had a thin dusting of moistness glazing its surface. The beast was muttering in a dialect only the beast would understand and was staggering around in circles at its own pace. You can't get lost when you have no place to go, I thought to myself.

I could feel the quantum click was coming again, though instead of waiting for the change to come, that was to take me to a place of the being's choice, I focused my thoughts and attempted to find reality. The being again spoke to me in a whisper of telepathy telling me to look to my feet. I glanced downwards and seen there were three large swellings on them. I felt like the being was trying to show me the answer is in the feet. I had no answer for the being at that moment out with time. I did not even have a question. I was lost.

As I came to consciousness, I found myself damp and shivering under the old decaying bridge where I'd slept for the night. I had been dreaming. The clock at the side of my cardboard bed was a steeple protruding out of a city in the distance. I could make out that it read exactly seven am. Sweat was leaking from every pore in my body. I rose from my dream and picked up a broken wing mirror out of an old discarded hold all. My eyes were a sea blue color, like they had the ocean living in them. I was sure the last time I'd looked they had been grey. They had always been grey...

The dream had been powerful. I felt as if I had just awoken for the first time in my life, everything appeared to be fresh and new, all of the little pieces of the world in front of me had a new glow and ambience around them. I was feeling new born to the same world. Something had changed. As my eyes fell to my feet, the swellings had disappeared though there were now three small scars on my foot as real as my foot itself. It had been real! What the hell? I lit a cigarette and drank the dregs of beer from last night's night cap. I began to feel lost. I thought of the dream. If I was lost, then there was some place I had to be going to, as you can't be lost unless there's some place you're going to. Only when I felt truly lost no more, would I have reached where I was meant to be, that is if I was meant to be anywhere at all. It was simple. I had to go and find this place. I had no idea what I was searching for though at least I knew I was searching for something. It was a start.

As I walked somewhat reluctantly towards the city and its intrinsic busyness, I looked back at the old bridge that had been my home for the night. I'd slept in worse places and no doubt I'd sleep in worse again. As I walked I sang a little song to myself and for any others who happened to be listening be it the breeze, the bees or the trees.

> "The sunshine, tells me I'll be just fine
> Yeah the sunshine, tells me I'll be just fine.
> So I walk another ridge and I cross another bridge
> And I do the journey slow
> Cause I got no place to go

Oh the sunshine tells me I'll be just fine.

When my heart breaks, I can feel my soul shake
Oh when my heart breaks, I can feel my soul shake
So I climb another tree and I swim another sea
Cause I got no chains on me
I'm enjoying being free
Oh when my heart breaks, I can feel my soul shake.

In a dream a girl walk by, she was looking to the sky
In a dream a girl walk by, she was looking to the sky
Well she knew me yesterday though she don't know me today
And I don't know reasons why
Though don't worry I won't cry
In a dream a girl walk by, she was looking to the sky.

And the morning bird sings, about so many different things
And the evening bird sings, about so many different things
And it soars up higher high to the kingdom in the sky
And if I were in its shoes
I guess that's just what I would do
And the birds sing, about so many different things."

The tune comforted me and raised my spirits. I continued my walk towards the city of Amsterdam.

Chapter Two

"So what choice of nature do you have?" I asked. "Any flavor you want my friend, any flavor you want", replied the vendor man. I settled on a small bag of some hybridized green that seemed good value and looked more potent than anything I had ever smoked before. I took my choice of nature, and the coffee that came free with my purchase, and took a seat near the back of the coffee shop. It was empty, though it looked as if this was a place that was used to that. It was around midday now and bright outside on the eyes. Inside the coffee shop it was darker, almost like dusk. I thought that it didn't matter how bright or dark it is if you're inside, when you're inside your inside, and when you're outside your outside, they are two very different places and each have their own set of guidelines.

Many different people had come and did exactly what I was doing at that very moment in that very place, though you can be doing the same job as the man next to you and be thinking on a completely different line. I rolled up the nature and sparked it. I used matches, as I've always preferred them to lighters. A lingering memory off hitting rock against rock to make fire was the ever reoccurring pleasure.

I began to start making some homemade juggling spheres as I sat smoking. It was one of my ways of making a little extra cash on the road when I had the chance. I used balloons, rice and plastic bags to make them. First I would cut off the lips of the balloons. Next I would fill a bag with rice. Then I would

19

pull the balloon over the bag of rice and finally I would pull over one more balloon in the opposite direction to complete the sealed sphere. On the street I would joke with the passersby that you got a meal with every sphere. They cost almost nothing to make and made me only a little extra cash, though sometimes it was enough.

"Do you have a light?" spoke a voice. I looked over my shoulder and was surprised to see that I was not alone in this dingy pocket in Amsterdam. There was an old man sitting in the shadows a few tables behind me doing exactly what I was doing, though he had a plate with a few biscuits sitting next to his coffee. He was dressed in a blue and green shirt and looked very settled.

"No bother" I said, and passed him the matches. The old man looked at the matches in his hand then passed them back.

"Better you give me the nature that is already alight don't you think?" I do think, I thought to myself. It was because I was lost in thought that I had missed this possible action. The man was right, there was no need to ignite another match when fire was already present so I passed him the lit nature and he lit his own chosen flavor.

"Do you know where fire came from?" asked the old man as he returned the light. It was a question I hadn't been asked before and I could find no answer, which the old man acknowledged. He continued...

"I heard it was born in a place in a time long before the earth existed on some other earth like planet, on some far out cosmical horizon. It's father was vengeance and it's mother was heartache.

In this place there once lived two animals, they were in love and wandered freely together in a world of vast mountainous forests. Every day they would hunt, rest and play together. Together, love was their most meaningful purpose and together, they felt balanced and happily complete. Then on one of these happy days like all the others they had spent together, they crossed a fallen tree that lay across a high crevice. The male animal's love fell into that crevice that day.

After much difficulty, the animal reached the bottom of the crevice and found the shattered broken body of his love. There was no life in his love and he realized now, there was no love in his life. The hand that had provided for his love for so long took a rock now, and all the animals confusions became the force behind its throw. The rock crashed against the side of the crevice, shattering it into a great number of pieces. The animal noticed that one of these pieces was alive for an instant. The animal had just created a spark and in that moment of distraction, his pain was gone. He had made the untouchable land that had taken his love from him bleed. If the land could bleed, thought the animal, then it could die and he wanted his revenge.

He was thinking only of what the land had taken from him and not all it had provided. He wanted more of this satisfaction and began to throw more and more rocks to ease his pain. With every spark came a moment of satisfaction as he was concerned with the spark and not his lost love. In his frenzy he failed to notice that a spark had lit the dead leaves and branches that had fallen into the crevice from the tree above, layering its floor. A fire rose and consumed the animal and his broken love."

"So his hunt for satisfaction ended him?" I asked "Yes. If he had accepted that when he seen the spark for the first time he had been satisfied, and that it was possible to feel satisfaction out with his love, he could have continued to develop that idea and rebuild his life. Blindly though, he repeated the same action again and again until there was so much of the same around him that the similarity consumed him".

If the animal had died in this event then how had the knowledge been passed on I thought, and as though the old man was reading my mind

"There are always eyes watching for new creations to pass on".

"Where are you going?" asked the old man. "To where I don't feel lost any more" I replied. "And do you feel lost now?" he asked. "Yes... I do". I had to continue my journey now I thought. "I cannot show you where to go or what to do when you get to this place you're searching for, though I can offer you a biscuit which will give you a little energy to help you get there. Thank you for the light and I wish you a safe journey. Remember that if something as big as fire had remained hidden until then, what else remains hidden until now!" I thanked the old man for the biscuit and also for the light he had given me, and went on my way.

Chapter Three

On leaving the coffee shop I went on my mission of finding my haven for the night. There was very little money in my pocket, which is more of a problem to some people than it is to others and it was often a problem for me. I hadn't been used to having a lot of money most of my days, though I didn't complain. It's difficult to truly miss something you have never truly had. I considered myself to be lucky for the life I had lived so far, the good and the bad included. It always seems much easier for things to become worse than it is for them to become better. 'As long as you have your health' my mother used to say. Having spent time without it I knew these words were wise.

I'd had jobs that made money though never stayed in them long enough to reach that safe place financially, I just liked to pick up the talent of the job and move on before I became the job. I'm not saying that's the right way to do it. It's just that's how it had been working out. I'd learned very early in life that I had to make what I could of every situation. When looking into the unpredictable still of moments to arrive, I was aware that sometimes you have to be opportunistic. I would hate to have had a chance and missed it, all because I was too scared to risk it. I enjoyed to converse with others that had been opportunistic or had made their own opportunities. These people held many keys. To look into the eyes of someone that is talking and reminiscing about a trip or a moment that they didn't miss, gave me hope. I had long enjoyed observing people simply closing their eyes and reliving their experiences when they so wished. I looked forward to the day when I too would have the sort of experiences that I could call upon to put a smile on my face or to pass on to another to help them through the present. I was aware that time was a hunter and that we cannot escape its kill, that someday we all had to accept its chill and that above all, surviving was living so to enjoy the thrill.

In my wander to find my haven, I found myself at the Central Train Station.

I saw an opportunity now. I took my backpack off and sat it next to me on the street. It was a trusty old backpack and had been with me for a long time on the road. It had become a friend. It was busy enough to grab a few pennies from the hands of the passer by, so I got out my clubs from my backpack and the spheres I had made in the coffee shop and began juggling. A while later I had enough cash to buy a ticket to some other place, although I was not going to buy a ticket unless I had to. I'd do the usual jump on the train and play my favorite 'avoid the ticket man' game.

I had no idea when or where the next train was or would be going, though I did know it was a train station with trains that go places, and that was enough of a sure thing. It was starting to get late so I jumped on a train that had the numbers 37 on the side and was just preparing to leave. The train pulled away from the station and as it did a man in his early twenties halted his rush to catch this train, as he realized he was too late. Our eyes met. He looked jealous. I felt lucky. The train built up speed and was soon trucking along at a fine pace. The colors of unseen places flashed in my eye as the train rolled on by them.

After 5 or 6 hours of night travel I got out of the train at Paris, still with my train ticket fare intact after several avoidance acts with the conductor. It was busy and sometime of early morning and there was a new haze of language in the air as the city began to rise and shine. It was not at all intimidating walking through the train door into this city of such reputation and as I immersed myself deeper into Paris I began to enjoy my walk immensely. All forms of art and architecture lined every street as if the city was built around each intricate part of the changed nature. There were countless statues and sculptures of people, of animals, of mystical beasts and there were even statues of the people that had made the statues and sculptures. The beauty of them and the work and personal struggles that must have went into them, was shining bright to my eye and penetrating my heart. It was a pleasure to absorb and be part of its offerings and a sure contented disposition rose over my face, which I passed on to many passersby on the streets of Paris that day.

As I began to tire from the effects of the travel and broken sleep, I found myself at the foot of the Eiffel Tower. The serenity of experiencing a place for the first time in person, of a place that has been seen so frequently in moments of life through other angles was intoxicating. It had that animated cartoon effect about it. I walked under the tower and took a seat on the grass in the park. The park stretched a fair distance until some larger buildings that whispered tales of the French revolution made the horizon against the blue sky.

I had a drink of the wine that I had bought from a man at a stall on the bridge over the river Seine, that I had just crossed to get here, and ate a little bread that I had acquired from the same source. I could notice the earth's roll as I gazed upward to the top of the tower and I laughed a little to myself as I noticed this. I often thought that laughter could be learning and not to forget the rock and roll of life was the laughter learning there. It was getting dizzy; "I'll blame that on the wine" I thought myself and laughed a little more.

In my haze, I hadn't been aware that a boy was standing next to where I was, sitting having a chuckle at my smiles. "Bonjour" I said to the lad, "Bonjour monsieur" he returned the hello. "A penny for a portrait" said the boy. "A portrait is surely worth more than a penny" I continued happily. "I thought you might say that and I'll hold you to it now monsieur", the boy smiled inwardly at his well-laid con and took out his paper and pastels from his satchel and began to draw. This was a wily little fellow to be sure.

The boy went about his job swiftly with ease though he did not seem to be looking directly at me, more around me, as he rolled his eyes back and forth from the paper. In hardly no time at all he spun the paper around, which had now become an interesting piece of changed nature and was a very well-drawn picture indeed. The face did resemble mine. He had drawn me hanging onto the tower like a flag blowing in the wind, with fish in the sky and a single dove sitting on the top most point of the tower. "That is how I seen you" said the boy, and he put out his hand for which I put a greater sum than a penny which had been somewhat unwittingly agreed as before on my behalf. "Merci and good luck with your talent". I thanked.

The boy smiled, gathered his tools and walked over to a young couple sitting under a tree, to continue working his talents. I looked at the portrait again and felt a calm breeze rise over me. I rolled up the drawing and stored it in my bag. I had surges of energy now and so decided to take to foot and concentrate this surge into the journey.

I found another busy street corner that became my office and made enough cash from the juggling to get drunk. I sold the remainder of the spheres I'd made in Amsterdam apart from four that I did not want to sell, and even managed to sell the picture the boy had drawn of me to a sock sandaled camera wearing tourist at a slight profit. Who's smiling now kid, I thought to myself. I just had to find a place that would suit my underlying alcoholic craving.

I had arrived in Paris with barely any money and I doubted I would leave it any better off. I would be just another cog to take part in its timing and keep the cities internal clock ticking. If I left it with anything of substance, other than more hazy memories and forgotten nights, it would be a bonus. A city can easily trap and eat you up without the slightest feeling of indigestion.

Walking along a narrow cobbled street lined with coffee

shops I heard a muffled saxophone oozing from a basement bar named 'The Brass Boulevard'. That should do the trick I thought. Time to go inside again. I'd heard about these places in Paris though I couldn't say I had given them much thought. I walked down the concrete stairway that was decorated with some beautiful flowering hanging baskets and went through the black door. I was faced with another black door. I went through it and was faced with yet another black door. The two doors behind had closed leaving me in darkness. I pushed through what was the last portal and finally entered the bar. I immediately understood the three-door system. Light would have killed the atmosphere. Inside, it looked and felt exactly like it would if I had attempted to create the scene in my mind based on expectations.

It was comfortably dark, smoky and lighted with candles, which sat on small round tables accompanied with a random scattering of chairs with a random scattering of people sitting on them. People dressed in black sat on black leather sofas lining the old stone walls, looking part of the furniture. The saxophonist sat on a stool next to a microphone on a raised stage in the far corner, and was highlighted by a soft red stage light. There was a piano and a set of drums waiting for attention next to him. The bar was retracted into the background and hidden in darkness. All I could make out was the silhouette of the bartender, the whites of his eyes and the glint of candlelight reflecting of the glasses and bottles on the shelves behind him. I walked towards the eyes. "Something strong and make it a double" I asked. I passed the eyes the money received my drink and change and went to take a seat. There didn't appear to be any groups so all seats were open. I took off my backpack and parked myself on a leather sofa sinking into its give, relaxed into the shadows and began to listen to the tunes.

Around three performers, a filled ashtray and a handful of doubles later, I felt right at home. The joint had got busy. A well-dressed young gent holding a black and silver rectangular case had taken a seat next to me midway through the second set. A disrespectful look and nose touch was his only reaction when he looked in my direction. Apart from this visual introduction we had not spoken to each other yet.

The latest set consisting of piano, sax, drums and double bass wound down and finished. Their end raised a light clapping and a few murmured comments from the audience.

"Look at them" hissed the well dressed gent next to me in a heavy French accent. He was commenting on the audience's tired reaction. "Unappreciative, unexcited, uninspired, unhappy. Waiting for something to happen though not knowing what it is they wait for. Nullified by another mediocre performance. Being part of the scene though doing no more. Crying out from behind their expressionless selves for something different." The gent turned and looked at me. "What's your purpose here gypsy? You're not helping this situation. You don't belong here. Why don't you get back on the street and play your role!" I looked the pretentious bastard in the eye. "Maybe I'm that something different you search for sir" I replied. The class monger looked at me in condescending disbelief. "Let me tell you gypsy, if you can change my world, I'll change yours". I looked down to the ground then back to his eye. "I don't like to tell, I could maybe show you", I replied in a more than relaxed whisky confidence manner.

"Then show me now" he hissed arrogantly. He reached down to his black and silver case, picked it up and sat it on his knee. He popped the case open to reveal a clarinet in two pieces. He picked up the two pieces and assembled them as if preparing pistols for a dual at dawn. He then stood up and took his ten paces, which brought him next to the microphone on stage, spun around to face me and fired. "Hello everyone let me give you an example of why the untalented waste of society disgusts me. Get up here gypsy" He pointed at me and all eyes turned towards his point. I stood up and picked up my bag to leave. I didn't want this. "You see. Another empty shell destined for hell."

I don't know why, but that outburst stopped me in my tracks. I dropped my bag and walked up to the stage. I turned and looked out at the audience. They were silent and sat in anticipation. I looked around at Mr. Clarinet. "Well...what you waiting for", I beckoned. There came four taps on the drumsticks and the music began. The drummer played a simple four beat and was complemented by the double bass. The piano delicately twinkled and danced around them. Mr. Clarinet slithered about in the gaps. I began to click my fingers to get into the beat.

"Get him off!" came a yell from the audience. I continued to click my fingers. "Get back inside the bottle". Came another shout. I continued to click my fingers. "Booooo" came a collective voice from a section near the leather seats. I grabbed the microphone out of its stand and began to sing.

"Living in the mission you desire
Living in the cataclysm of the fire
If hates what warms your heart we're worlds apart
The power surge to heal the urge the separation start
Destroy yourself; give means to stealth
become the camouflage
Create the scene from way beyond the screen
free spirit soar at large"

The clarinet cut in. I looked to my left and could see Mr. Clarinet was trying to put me off.
I listened to the beat of the drums and focused
on the baseline. I began to click my fingers
again to the beat and found the rhythm.

"Idols fall when you get a little higher
Offerings try to catch out choke the liar
Burn a copy if you need the tricks to get the fix
Do not be tame it's all just a game this oceans full of clicks
If you want to be a player maybe got to be a sayer
Got to venture to the layer of the solitary slayer"

Mr. Clarinet again broke through my rhythm with a deliberately timed cut. Then came a yell from the audience directed at Mr. Clarinet. "Give the music a chance". I looked over at Mr. Clarinet. I clicked my fingers and got back into the beat.

> "Where I am from all I can say is I don't know
> Be it country, religion or race how far back will I go
> Now you're looking at me and I'm looking at you
> No need for the answers when the questions ain't true
> And the flowing fountain from natural mountain
> is surely something to be
> And the invisible winds blowing from within
> surely something to see"

Mr. Clarinets timing was sublime. There was a change in the clarinets flow. Its sound was playing with me now. He was supporting me when my voice weakened and returning to the shadows when I was peaking. I looked to the side. Mr. Clarinet was lost in the music. The audience was there as well. There was no booing, only collective creation as they all clicked along to the rhythm.

> "Break from the mold let the journey unfold
> Hell, heaven, breathe, dying and living are
> all breakable codes
> The dreams feel more real, the real is always more surreal
> The makers the takers the breakers the steal and the wheel
> The age the wage turn the page the server and the served
> The judges the nudges the grudges let all be reserved"

The place was jamming. Everyone in the bar was feeling it. I had to go now. Leave on the high. I'd played my part. I walked off the stage and moved through the crowd towards the exit, picking up my bag with a series of handshakes and back pats on the way. I passed through the three-door system to find it was around late evening time. I made my way up the stairway towards the cobble street. "Wait up friend!" I turned around to see Mr. Clarinet had followed me outside. The music still continued in the bar. "I said if you could change my world, I'd change yours. Take this and thank you." He passed me an envelope and went on back inside. I heard Mr. Clarinet start up again from within the Brass Boulevard. I'd made someone's day so I went on my way.

It was dark now, there had been a shower of rain and the cobbled pathway was glazed with moistness. Due to winding down from the whisky and impassioned improvisation, words kept coming to my mind and spilling out of my mouth resulting in me muttering away as I walked along the street. I stopped and looked up. I wondered why I was going this way. I turned around and began walking back along the street. I stopped again and again thought of why I was going this way. I felt lost. I was struck with a bolt of déjà vu. I remembered the dream of the beast staggering around in circles muttering in a dialect only the beast would understand. You can't get lost when you have no place to go I remembered. I felt lost. I must have somewhere to go. I looked at the envelope in my hand and opened it. Inside was a flight voucher worth 400 euros! This was the key I had dug up. I had to get out of this city now *before it took it back.*

Chapter Four

I heard a bird sing from some green bushes nearby, I was sitting at ease with a warm sun on my face. There was an improvised plant pot on either side of me made out of some old whisky barrels that were green with moss. The pot to my left contained three plants which I made out to be a nettle, a bramble with berries and a Docan leaf plant which were all looking as healthy and as full of life as each other. The pot to my right was full of several beautiful flowering plants of varied form. I reached to the pot on the left to pick a juicy dark purple berry from the bramble though as I did this, the nettle plant stung me. I had learned as a child that the Docan leaf with a bit of saliva was the natural balance to a nettle sting, so I removed a leaf from the Docan plant, spat and rubbed it on the sting, which instantaneously brought me some relief. There was a certain yin and yang feeling to the action. I was more careful this time and picked three berries from the bramble and ate them. The berries were sweet and succulent and I spat the seeds back into the soil of the plant pots. I noticed that the soil in both the plant pots was dry and in need of moisture. There happened to be a jug of water and a jar of honey next to me, so I took up the jar of water and gave each pot a good drink. For some reason I felt that the plants were all a little happier after that and I felt contented that I'd had some part to play in their daily struggle.

I looked around and saw that I was in a clearing surrounded in trees, in that I could describe my surroundings as a forest, though I was aware that each tree had its own unique glow around it. The sun was high in the sky and its light was a gently blown kiss of orange softly oozing through the canopy. The only clouds I could see were encircling the sun like the mane of a dreaming sky lion, with a gentle breeze flowing through the forest that would be its sleepy breath.

A small buzz came to my ear; I pinpointed its source to be emitting from a small honeybee just a few yards before me. It appeared to be in distress, so remembering about the jar next to me, I scooped a little of the sweet honey with my finger and fed it to the bee, who lapped it up ravishingly. I sat back, licked my fingers clean of honey with great satisfaction and watched the bee slowly regaining its strength as it lapped up the last of the honey. When the honey was finished the bee appeared rejuvenated and began to clean itself preparing for flight. Its wings began to rotate and soon became a blur accompanied by that familiar buzz. It raised itself of the ground a little shakily at first, though was in control in no time. It began to circle in the air, though did not fly away and continued circling a few yards ahead of me faster and faster. I began to feel a little uncomfortable as its buzz became louder and louder as it spun around faster and faster and I became mesmerized by this motion of sound and color. The circle of its flight path had become a ring that made it look as if there were more than one bee there creating a ring of Saturn effect. Suddenly the blurred circle became a bow and shot an arrow of color and sound heading straight for my eye. I could not close my eyelids and the arrow of bee struck true into my eye.

I jumped and gave out a yell, and as I opened my eye the bee was there in front of me again. "It's ok", came a soothing voice. "It's on the other side of the window, you're quite safe"

As I gathered myself together from my dream and looked around, I found that I was on the train that I had taken out of Paris. Looking out of the window that I'd been sleeping against I could see the bee was gone.

The area around was spectacular, becoming quite mountainous and the train was heading further into the raising gradient at an easy pace. "Are you here to climb the mountains?" asked the soothing voice. I turned to face the voice. I was taken aback at first because the voice belonged to a girl whose beauty surpassed that of the immense scenery we moved through. Her eyes were bright and dark with endless depth, her hair was long with thick dark ringlets that resembled a great cascading waterfall in the night. Her skin was a soft brown and flawless, with passion pink lips and a nose that looked to have been shaped through smelling the sweetest flowers of a distant kingdom. She blushed a little, as it was apparent that she could see my thoughts. I had not been prepared to see this apparition of beauty that sat next to me. Even if I had been pre warned of this moment and had trained a poker face for years, there was no hiding the truth of my amazement. "Well?" she continued. "Well" I retorted, for my shock at this sight left me without the capabilities of comprehensible speech. "Are you here to climb the mountains?" she repeated with a calming smile coming to her face. "Why would I want to do that?" I asked. She thought a little before replying to this

question. "Would you not want to do it because you need to do it?", "What's the difference" I intrigued.
"There are many things in life that you will want, and only a few that you will need. You need food because it is a necessary energy your body requires to live. It is not a want it is a need, though you will want and that's ok...everyone has a soul that compliments the body. Though the food your soul needs is different. The food of the soul is the way you live your life. As I said there are many things you will come across that you will want in life. Those that are just wants will be forgotten about, though some wants will continue to show themselves to you through everyday life and dreams. These pure wants are actually your true needs and you must reach these to nourish your soul, just as you must reach for bread to nourish your body. It is a daily process of moments that will nourish your soul, do you follow?" Having just woken up from a broken 'train sleep' I wasn't exactly on form for such an insightful conversation, though it did seem to make some sort of sense so I just gave an agreeably curious animal "hmm". "So do you want to go to the mountain or do you need to go?" I thought for a moment and replied "I didn't plan to come to the mountains; I only felt that this train was the best choice I had in the moment." "Which brought you to the mountains?" "Yes", "Then you do need to go to the mountains, if it was a true need you followed to bring you here". This girl was definitely crazy, a good type of crazy and I kinda liked that. "My name is Arico, what's yours?" "It's Zia". What a beautiful name it was. "How did you come to learn this Zia?" I asked

"Must have caught something in the wind". She smiled.

Chapter Five

"This feels like the stop" "Our start you mean?" Zia replied with a spark. We saddled up our rucksacks and hopped of the train. The station wasn't busy; there was a few people with various climbing tools with soon to be or had been frosted beards and woolly hats drinking plastic coffee out of plastic cups. The only other character was a short podgy fellow, wearing a buttons style uniform that stood to attention behind a cardboard cutout desk, wallpapered with tourist, moth to light offers.

How many days had it been since I had last eaten in Paris? I had a hunger that would have suggested it had been many days since my last meal. "Let's find some food and a haven to prepare for the trek." Zia suggested. "We're flowing on the same wavelength Zia....what do you mean by a trek?" Zia just rolled her eyes "Come on space tripper". I hadn't planned to go on any trek, then again, I hadn't been planning anything and this was where my itchy feet had brought me which I could accept. I quickly decided to synchronize my movement with her. She seemed to be working on a good idea and I felt comfortable trusting her.

This was a majestic village so closely in touch with the sky. The snowcapped mountains ran off into the beyond, surrounding this enchanting oasis. The clear blue was fading as we searched for food and was slowly being replaced by a deeper dark. A twinkle of light from a distant star shone in my eye reminding me that the moon was chasing away the sun and

41

darkness would arrive soon. I noticed Zia had a tent strapped to the bottom of her rucksack. I suggested we should find a market and a place to camp to take advantage of the tools we had at our disposal. In reality, I was broke and the high priced bar/restaurant scene of Chamonix was thankfully out with my budget and would surely be a little more interesting than pretentious cocktails with the rich. Maybe I was a little harsh on 'the rich'. It's nobody's fault what their born too. I knew I shouldn't try to hide my lack of money from Zia as she seemed the sort of soul that could see beyond these things. There was a hint of male animal pride messing with me with the addition of knowing that getting a camp fire on the go and sleeping under canvas simply blows the bar scene out of the water. Zia agreed, and by the fall of night we had the tent pitched with some pasta boiling away in a mess tin.

We had set up camp near a stream in the forests at the foot of the mountains. I turned the fish that was smoking above the camp fire we had made from some gathered firewood and then sat back with a smoke ourselves. I became entirely relaxed. The night had come now and had brought the stars with it. The dark became an ideal velvet blanket displaying the jewels of the night in remarkable splendor. I invented a new word to attempt to describe its beauty as I felt I had not the word within my own verbal dictionary. The word was zanical and it truly was a zanical evening. I wondered if I had the right to invent a new word. I'd heard the phrase before that if something can't be said better than it's already been said, say it that way, though if it can be said a better way, then say it that way. I decided I did have a right to at least make new attempts. Either way, it did appear more zanical than any other word in my possession.

The meal was ready and looked delicious. We were both ravenous and the smoked fish was a tasty accompaniment to the pasta, moist with a sauce of chopped tomatoes mixed with a local mountain herb.

"You only eat fish and vegetables Arico? That's the same diet I follow, I'm interested to ask for your reasons why you have chosen this way". It was a simple question I had been asked often and my answer always seemed to vary. "I seem to have more reasons why I shouldn't eat some animals than why I should. There are some things I want to be part off and some things I don't. I had once had a job cleaning out an old chicken farm. There were dead chickens amongst the sawdust in the pens that were as thin as a wafer because the conditions had been so cramped that they had been trampled to death, compressed by the weight of the other chickens. I don't want to eat battery chickens or eat battery eggs because I'm fueling the need and helping its system exist. I swore I would not be a part of that circle any more after that experience. Surely there is another way!". "And do you think that vegetables or fish are treated any better when they are farmed or caught?" asked Zia, I thought about this question. "Hell no Zia" "Then are you sure that's the reason why you only eat fish and vegetables?" Of course Zia was right, as there was no consistency in my reason though does reason require consistency? "I guess a lot of the time it's based on circumstance and choice. If I was a lion or a fly or a starfish or a tree, my outlook would certainly be different and I count myself lucky that I have had at times the luxury of choice. I mean if necessity requires it, you do what you have to just to survive, whether that's killing a fellow animal, picking fruit of a tree or pulling up a rooted vegetable. Plants are living organisms too; maybe because they don't have a nervous system it's easy to believe that they feel no pain, though they certainly have systems...They have a will to survive! Why else would a thorn bush have thorns? Like how a rhino has horns, there is something there that life feels is worth protecting...I've went through periods where at times I haven't eaten for days because I was so concerned with the reasons behind what I was consuming. What a brutal world this is though we can't live off air...though sometimes I wish we could. The world would be a simpler place. What are your reasons? " I asked in the hope she could make it all very clear all very quickly "It feels like the correct choice for me, though like you I'm still unsure as to the true reasons why. I'm sure it will be revealed to me at some point." Her relaxed and honest eyes melted me. "Your inspiring me to believe it will be Zia". "Do you think that could be why we have met?" asked Zia. "What do you mean" I wondered. "Maybe our diets have put us on a similar path. Say I was a koala bear and you were a panda. It's unlikely we would have met, seeing as I would need to be near eucalyptus trees and you would have to be near bamboo, which grow in different environments." I thought about it for a moment. "I kind of see what you mean. Because the food we search for is found in the same environments...

We'll be found in the same environments." "Yes. By eating fish and vegetables it seems we're quite lucky to find each other, seeing as we could have met anywhere on the land, anywhere in fresh water or anywhere in the sea" , "Or anywhere in the cosmos...". She laughed at this. I was happy about that even though it was a shit joke but laughter's learning right? ...Got to love even a shit sense of humor when things start getting pretty deep, it helps you keep a sense of depth.

The meal was finished and our bellies were full. Our camp fire was a deep warm ember of orange which was soothing me towards sleep. We left the fire to fade in its own time and got into the tent, cozying up together in our sleeping bags.

I closed my eyes to smile and enjoy the contentment of the company. I loved the road and traveling ways. One moment I'm waking alone under a cold bridge, the next I'm sleeping next to a beautiful woman up a zanical mountain. When you're up, enjoy it ... and when you're down, don't get too down.

"I have one more question to ask before we sleep Arico". I did not open my eyes and still wore the warmth of this life on my face as I rolled my head towards Zia to beckon her to continue. "I noticed earlier your reaction to the prices of the hostels and restaurants we passed, it's clear that you don't have much money which is no issue, though it fuels my question which is to wonder how you can afford to travel. On hearing this I became lightened for I knew the answer, and it was a simple one. Still without opening my eyes I gave her the answer. "I juggle". The last sound I heard of the night was Zia's mirth at my answer.

Chapter Six

I was high up in the sky; underneath me I could see a sea of vast green and I was floating above it. I did not have any wings and could not understand how I was in control of my flight. Doubt started to break the illusion and I began to fall towards this mass of green. The cold grasp of panic set in as the green came closer. As I fell closer I seen it was not a green sea but a great rainforest. As I broke through the upper canopy a branch protruded from this green mass which somehow I managed to grab in some 16th chapel divine Da Vinci moment. The branch began to fold and as it reached breaking point, I began to feel light again and catapulted back into the air. From this bird's eye view, I could see that I was flying over the top of the grandest of rainforests that stretched to the horizon. When I realized this and began to doubt the reality, I began to fall again. This time when I touched down on the green upper canopy there was no divine branch to grab and I did not feel light and launch back into the air... I began to fall deeper into the underlying canopy. As I fell, I grabbed at the branches available and managed to latch onto one, swinging myself onto a thick branch next to the trunk avoiding what felt like some impending collisional doom. I sat perched on the branch under the canopy of green. Below me was also green, though it got darker and looked as if it was night due to the upper canopy halting the light from reaching the depths of the rainforest floor.

The music of a bird singing came to my ear. I looked to my left

to see a small blue and green bird perched next to me. I began
to listen to its song. At first it sounded only beautiful, though
I could not understand what the song was about. I focused on
the sound and out of the static of non-understanding, came
words to this bird's song.

"And I'm trying to wonder how this can be
Sitting peaceful in the shade of another canopy
And the angel says your quite today
Just listening to the deafening sounds of silence and its ways
And I'm trying to wonder how this can be
All the beauty that surrounds is a blanket that is free
Heat of comfort smothers getting to warm
Got to bank this fragile moment keep ahead of static swarm
And I'm trying to wonder how this can be
Was not ready for the shout, been awoken to early
And I fall into the wells of the say
Fill the bucket from my soul, which whispers songs
of a practice day
And I'm trying to wonder how this can be
Got no new tricks for expectations that's the
lesson you should see
Don't conjure up falseness put words to my lips
I could be dreaming of unknown, or of all the
unmissed trips
And I'm trying to wonder how this can be
Breathe a voice into the shadow and fulfill a destiny
Return to life alive, in body and mind

> The journey was worth all the pain for the
> treasures we did find"

At this; the green and blue bird flew out through the canopy leaving me alone on the branch. I heard a crack as the branch I perched on began to break.
I closed my eyes and as I closed them to this world my eyes opened and I found myself lying in the tent next to Zia.

It had been another dream...

The night had paced by with ease. There had been a certain freshness in the air that night that made me thankful for the shelter of the tent. The warmth of the two bodies close to each other more than kept the cold at bay, leaving me refreshed and energized when I woke. Zia still slept so I calm breezed out of the tent and set off to get some water for the morning coffee.
The surroundings in morning light had the knock on effect of filling me with the same light that touched all that my hungry eye could find. Millions of years in the making and that eye was still making! The mountain peaks formed a circular horizon of green with glistening white peaks whispering their presence beyond them. Glaciers perched on the green mountains resembling mammoth icy fingers reaching and extending from the mass of distant white, the barrier of green appearing only to slow the ices inevitable stretch.
A stream sourced from one of these icy fingers, flowed a short

distance behind where we had set camp. It was the same stream that I'd collected the water from last night to boil the pasta in and it was only now that I realized this melting glacial water could easily be thousands of years old which probably wasn't a good thing. It was too late now anyway and I felt fine having already drunk from it the previous night. I just tried to see it as a fine aged whisky!

As I reached it, I bent to my knees and decided to submerge my head in the stream, which seemed like a good idea until it was done. The feeling was so awakening I had to jump around shaking and holding my head as if my entire head had just become a huge sensitive tooth that had just bitten ice cream. The easy haze of last night's sleep disappeared as full awakening took over. Filling the mess tin I returned to the camp to find Zia still sleeping so I lit the fire and put the water on the boil. I reached into my pack to find some breakfast biscuits though as I did this a juggling ball was disturbed and fell to the ground. I may as well have a juggle while the coffee brews I thought.

I had been juggling most of my life. My grandfather showed the talent to me and I have in turn passed it on to many others who wished to learn the trade.

I remember the story my grandfather told me of how he learned of juggling in the world wars. As a boy his stories of the war had me spell bound and his introduction to juggling was a favorite. A fellow of the name Jamma passed juggling to my grandfather in the trenches of Normandy. The fellow's real name was Wilson. For reasons long forgotten he was known in his unit, including to the officers as simply Jamma.

My grandfather was stationed with Jamma in a trench on the front line. He recalled that they were pinned down under heavy fire, with bullets and mortar shells raining a deadly hail in this metallic storm of death. The mortars were close range and dug in a mere two hundred yards or so in front of them. They were causing devastating damage wreaking havoc on my grandfather and Jamma's unit, the radio man being an early casualty. In the confusion of battle they found themselves cut off with little more choice than to sit tight and 'eat the dirt' until either it relented, they got support or given their situation and most likely conclusion, they were killed.

A mortar shell crashed and exploded just a few yards from their position covering them in dirt, which wounded and shell shocked my grandfather, causing him permanent deafness in his right ear. My grandfather described shell shock as being sober then instantly becoming heavily drunk without being able to sleep through the hangover. As the dust began to clear, my grandfather still in shock rolled over to face Jamma. To my Grandfather's continued shock, through his blurred vision he saw Jamma standing bolt upright in the cloud of dust, stripped down to only his combat trousers and boots juggling three hand grenades! He glanced towards my grandfather and spoke the words "Juggling can save", which in my grandfather's state he could not have possibly heard though he swears he heard Jamma's word clear and true. With those words Jamma strode over the trench top juggling the three grenades, disappearing into the engulfing cloud of smoke which flashed and hissed like a fiery tempest serpent. Jamma was never seen again. The mortar fire ceased.

When my grandfather returned home on medical leave, he made a report of the trench events. The army promptly swept the story under the rug and labeled my grandfather 'trench mad', discharging him on permanent medical terms. The army listed Jamma as 'Killed In Action' as his dog tags and shirt lay in a bloody mess next to where my grandfather was found, stating mortar fire most probable cause of death. My grandfather knew the truth though and has never forgotten Jamma's moment. Soon after returning home he began to juggle and was soon passing the talent on to many others, I had been one of those others.

"That's quite a talent you have", the unexpected voice startled me causing me to drop the juggling spheres. One of the spheres narrowly missed the over boiled pot of coffee while another's spiraling descent collided with some hot embers, sending up feather light sparks from the morning camp fire. The voice belonged to Zia, who was now sitting at the entrance of the tent. "It's just another language I speak" I said, "Like English or Spanish you mean?" asked Zia "Or French, science, guitar or car even. It's a language I enjoy speaking". Zia contemplated for a moment, "Then can you teach me to speak this language Arico?", "I surely can and will enjoy to do so only we mustn't learn here, we must learn there", Zia's eyes turned to where I was pointing and as she realized I was pointing at the glacier up the mountain, a daring wildness rose across her face. Then let's have the coffee and go!

Chapter Seven

As the morning sun had risen over the glistening glacier way up the green mountains, the vision had resembled a majestic white parrot with bright yellow head feathers seeming untouchable and unreachable.

After hiking all morning we now stood looking back down the valley from that great parrot's eyes at where we had spent the night. We had reached the glacier that had been the source of the stream that had made our morning coffee. The stream now looked like an endless flowing vein of life, meandering and disappearing along the valley. Under our feet was a frozen river of ice held in stasis. The same feeling that I'd felt at the Eiffel tower hinted at me as I thought of how strange it was to look at a place, and then be at that place looking out from it at the place you had just come from. It felt like realizing dreams and was enlightenly simple. I was liking this can see, can do way and wondered how far you could go learning to be fluent in this can see, can do language. "How does it feel?" asked Zia, "It's zanical Zia, such a pleasure to be, such a pleasure to see, letting the beauty of its energy come to we like the food to a tree. I'm so energized feeling part of this view shining bright to the eyes of the others standing where we stood last. I know that place is beautiful and this is also so I'm getting double the energy" "Hey space tripper, about the juggling?" Zia was beaming. The colors, the sound, the motion, I was in an ocean. An ocean of air and ice and ground, and it was as

deafening as silence though silence is a sound, I was tuned in to the silence and it was loud. All the pieces of surrounding life felt bound together like a hand linked crowd. What I could feel was like my feet were to come off the ground. "It's so silent and peaceful it's like music Arico. May I recite a poem to you I wrote when I was younger that reminds of now."
I looked at Zia. She was like a dream to me. I felt like I was falling in love. She began to speak.

>"I was sitting my perfect place
>With a bird on my shoulder
>Looking at heaven
>I looked at the river and I started to think
>I wish I could be a crocodile
>I thought a little more
>I did not wish to be a crocodile
>I saw two birds flying together
>And I wished I could be a bird
>And fly far, far away
>Though why fly far, far away
>When I'm already in my perfect place
>I thought of the two birds
>Could this be the place they fly to?
>When they fly far, far away
>Then I thought that I had been a bird
>And I had flown far, far away
>To my perfect place
>And my memories of life

> Had been my passing over dream
> And the bird on my shoulder
> The reminder"

A sound began to involve itself in the moment and as our ears caught the sound and its consequence became apparent, it was too late! I was weightless though in motion, a whirlpool of white aqua blue and brightly clothed arms and legs span to my eye, then all was dark, calm and still.

I woke to find myself on a ledge of ice no more than a few yards wide. Below the ledge was the darkness of an endlessly deep drop; in front were walls of darkness. The only source of light shone from the small hole in the ice which we'd fallen through. The walls of smooth sheer ice surrounding me were un-climbable. I could not see Zia so called her name into the dark for only the echo to return her name. A rush of pain from my ankle was followed by a rush of fear which gripped and stiffened my body. As I took stock of my injuries and slowed my breathing, I found that I was not badly injured bar a slight sprain of my ankle. My trusty rucksack had been tied firm to my back and had absorbed most of the impact and had surely saved my life. There was no way off this ledge in the abyss; I was going to have to wait. Maybe Zia is ok and has gone for help or maybe another climber will pass by, though I could not shout too loudly for help in the fear of causing an avalanche. I began to think of how difficult it would be to notice a small hole in the ice. I felt swallowed and the thought of slowly digesting in the darkness was an unbearable reality.

The light from the hole above barely illuminated the ledge. Soon the light and its relative warmth would be gone and replaced by the chilling cold of night.
I took off my backpack to forage for anything of use. As I did this a juggling sphere rolled free and almost fell into the darkness before my hand found it in mid fall. A special luminous material I'd sown around the sphere for night juggling still held enough light in its seams to glow through the dark. I decided I should juggle.

Chapter Eight

The hospital room was cold and sterile. The constant beep of the life support machines continued uninterrupted. A lady of dark features lay motionless on the only bed in the room. She was connected to the machine through translucent tubes, which pumped blood and water like a body distillery. A door opened and two men in white coats entered, closing the door gently behind them. "This is the unknown walker sir?" spoke a young voice "Yes Antoine" spoke a more authoritative tone. "She was found seven days ago lying unconscious in a stream near the tree line on the eastern slopes. She appears to have slipped and fallen into the stream, receiving blows to the head." "Will she remember anything if she wakes?" "It's hard to tell. If she wakes...her memory may be affected, but there have been no signs of her regaining consciousness. She is at least stable now." The younger doctor took the hand of the woman "Was she alone?" "It appears so. So far nobody has come forward with any information. A search party combed the area before they were forced to stop due to the snow storm that appeared. They found no trace or signs that she was with anyone else. If there was someone else in trouble I doubt they would have survived the storm. It's been seven days without a sound. Raise her eyelids and check her pupil dilation please Antoine, I need to go check on some other patients" The older doctor left the room. As Antoine lifted the eyelids of the woman, he was faced with the blank gaze of coma ....though it was changing. A spark of life shot through her pupils as she came alive. Antoine jumped back in shock scattering his notes over the plastic black and white checked floor. The woman squirmed and wriggled uncontrollably causing the tubes to break free, spilling and spraying bodily fluids on the floor defacing Antoine's notes. A nurse ran into the room and they managed to administer the woman with a shot that took almost instant effect. She became calm and gradually began to regain awareness and control.

"Where am I?" asked the woman "You are in the central hospital Lille, there's been a lot of people worrying about you. What's your name dear?" "It's Zia, what's yours?" "My names Antoine, I'm a student doctor here, "Where's Arico?" asked Zia "You were found alone" Replied Antoine. Zia pulled herself up to a sitting position. "We must get to the glacier".

I had lost count of how long I had been entranced in the juggle. I was singing quietly to myself as I juggled though the lyrics were becoming more and more delirious.

> "What ever happened to my soul,
> what ever happened to my rock and roll?
> The days go by I've lost my friends,
> I've got my health so I can make amends
> And it's all just the same in the end;
> it's all just a sin in the end
> There's no end and that is the end,
> it takes all to make a world
> What ever happened to the sky,

whatever happened to flying so high?
My feet are still upon the ground,
the sand is dropping I can hear the sound
Whatever happened to my soul,
part of the rock and I can feel the roll
The days go by I've found my friend,
I've joined it now have I made amends?
And it's all just the same in the end; i
t's all just a sin in the end
There's no end and that is the end,
it takes all to make a world
The moon chases the sun,
the sun chases the moon
The moon chases the sun don't it look like fun
They will meet up some day for a while they will stay
Then again go away on a different play
It goes dark when they meet sheltered from all the heat
It's gonna hurt you my friend that's why they call it the end
The fire between them intense the crowd
they watch with suspense
A joke at their own expense and out the window goes sense
The dark fades from the light making day out of night
The fires of earth re-ignite,
now continue the fight
The sun chases the moon the moon chases the sun
The sun chases the moon and they'll meet again soon
And they'll meet again soon,
and they'll meet again soon

> And they'll meet again soon,
> and they'll meet again soon."

The abyss consumed me. The juggling spheres had become a blur of light. The light from the illuminating material was having the knock on effect of lighting the other spheres forming a constant light. The faster I juggled the more intense the light became. I juggled faster and faster and the light became more intense and pure until all that I juggled was light. The cavern of ice came alive with color as a bolt of light catapulted from the juggle into a natural ice prism spreading spectrums of light in laser beams, bouncing across the icy walls shining up through the frozen ceiling towards the sky above.

A train pulled into Chamonix station. Zia hobbled of the train supported by Antoine. A crew made up of doctors and mountain rescue were waiting in the station and warmly greeted their arrival. "Do you remember where you were climbing Zia?" asked Antoine. Chamonix was white with snow. The blizzards had blown for seven days and nights covering all previous tracks, resetting the roads, pathways and landscapes making them appear untouched and settled for centuries. "I can't.... I can't remember, it all looks so different with the snow. Zia looked at her hands, they were feeling strangely warm. She turned her hands away and they suddenly cooled. She turned them once more and a sensation of heat was felt again. What was happening thought Zia. She followed the direction of where her hands pointed. Her eye caught a faint beam of light from a mountain to the east and a smile rose to her face.

"He's there!"

Chapter Nine

"How is it possible Arico? You should have frozen." I had no one answer for Zia. They had told me I had been on that ledge for 7 days. "I can only remember the juggling Zia". Somehow I had been kept in the moment through juggling and the change in the moment came to me. "The mountain rescue officer told me that you would not speak to them when they found you and refused to get checked up at the hospital", "I don't like uniforms or hospitals...any way it's not important", Zia was becoming impatient "Then what is Arico?", "I was entranced in the juggle, which may be as dangerous as it is wonderful. I had never been in a juggle for as long as that and do not know how long it could be continued. In my trance, many thoughts came and went like passing clouds. I remember the clouds of thought becoming a whirlwind and all was calm as I stood with firm feet in the eye of the motion. I looked upwards and there were stars above me, as I reached for them they were just out of reach. I continued to reach and my fingertips appeared closer though they were still out of reach. I went up on to my tiptoes like a ballerina, and got a little closer though the stars seemed just out of reach. I began to jump and bounce in a frenzied river dance reaching for the stars though they remained out of reach. I came to rest and stood once more in the calm of the motion. My hands were warm and I looked in the direction they faced. There was a clear calm pathway to the stars. I could see a jungle fading into sand, the sand faded into a crystal aqua blue sea that merged with a clear blue sky, darkening to a haze of new colors peppered with stars. I looked back from this image at my feet, I realized that no matter what mountain top I go to, my feet will still be on the ground only reaching, clambering and jumping from the ground. I saw that this could only end with becoming the ground. The sea was the gateway, and life's obstacles were the gatekeepers. Don't look at where you're going, look at where you want to be and can see can do will bring it to you." I paused and looked to the ground before looking into Zia's eyes.

"I must go now Zia, this place will be too full of questions on how I survived", "Then stay and answer them Arico" I bowed my head again. "I'm not sure I can yet, I have to move on". "Hey space tripper, you haven't taught me to juggle yet!" I raised my head and looked into Zia's eyes. "You have witnessed it, it's in you now, and it's only for you to convince yourself you can do it, if you choose too". Zia contemplated this for a moment. "Then thank you for teaching me to juggle." Zia was struggling to hold her posture so I shouldered her weight and held her true. "You must rest, these people will help heal you" "I can take care of myself"; she said proudly "Then let them care for you also and you will heal even sooner, use your travel insurance get outta jail card." Zia attempted to laugh though the pain was too much, smoothing her laugh to a smile. "Your train will be leaving soon space tripper." "Zia, we see the same sun and moon every night and day, so you can be the sun and I'll be the moon and sure enough our eclipse will come. You are not a dream, though I will dream of you". It was time to get to an airport and use the key I had dug up in Paris.

Chapter Ten

"Black coffee and an ashtray please". The waitress disappeared and returned with an ashtray and a box of complimentary matches. Your coffee will return in our next moment spoke her expression. I would always have my coffee black. I didn't drink milk. I remember seeing the sculpture of Romulus and Remus suckling the teats of the mother wolf. I saw drinking milk from a cow was basically the same. Maybe when it comes from a carton you're not exactly going underneath the cow directly, though if you go back to the source that's exactly what you are doing. It took a long time in design for a cow's milk to help its calf grow into a strong cow. I was not trying to grow into a strong cow so I didn't drink its milk. In saying that, there have been times when I have reverted back to its almost instantaneous nourishment and grounding feeling

I looked at the matches next to the ashtray. I remembered what the old man had said to me in the Amsterdam coffee shop. I looked around and saw a man at a table nearby already smoking. "Can I have a light bro?" I asked, "Sure can man" he replied. As he reached to his pocket I stopped him, repeating the old man's words, "Better to give me the light that is already present". The fellow duly obliged and passed on the lit flame like the Olympic torch at just as graceful a level. "Your right man, you gotta recycle it, and never quit" he chirped. This character bubbled with energy and beckoned me to sit and share the table with him.

The waitress arrived, and on noticing I had moved seats, brought my coffee over.

"A coffee and a smoke, how monotonous it is yet every time it seems a little different though I find it can be a comforting camouflage." said the man. "So that's why you smoke?" I asked. "Oh I know why I smoke. It has long been noted that trees and plants of all supposed types are living breathing animals just the same as any walker, flyer, swimmer or floater. They are almost stationary, in that I mean it comes to them quicker than they go to it for sure. To live the plants need food. We are their food. They need our bodies to become the nutrient soup of the ground, which is their hunting ground. The plants have many methods of reaching the same goal, none more ingenious than the tobacco plant. He is indeed a hero and giving savior of the plant world. The war we fight every day seems valid from each group's point of view, though the neutral watcher surveys a different story.

Enraged at all the destruction of the plant world by the humans, the tobacco plant made an elective choice to fight back and produce a fruit that people would be addicted to, that would damage them and bring them to the ground just a little quicker. No prisoners to the addicted! They produced a fruit that would be considered a necessity; a way for the mud sea to whisper its siren song, enticing the sheep to its ranks for addiction is no more than falsified need. Have we not learned from the dinosaurs? To become the ground is maybe not the way to go. As was said, it is a hero to its plant counterparts, as it doesn't directly benefit from the bodies that become the ground. They all don't drop dead within the tobacco plants roots or reachable hunting ground. Many bodies drop far away from their territory and produce food for many other needing plants, in turn getting the tobacco plant its legendary status among the plant world. It is this self-sacrifice, hit miss tactic that has made it such a hero. This plant has even infected the minds of many to help them grow and tend to their children in the form of tobacco nurseries and plantations. Happy they are to be farmed for they know the gift of their sacrifice!

The coffee plant is a close friend of the tobacco plant and they together formed a strong alliance to provide for their own kind. They saw a space and established themselves in it. Had they only stopped to see that they only fuelled the war of survival could they have found another way. Though that other way is not our reality as we sit here enjoying our smoke and coffee...

This is after all a carnivorous world we live in, a choice that occurred a long while ago and the consequence of it, to feed and be fed on by another. This is a reality you must be aware of!" I liked the way the guy thought although on quick contemplation surely the tobacco plant was already a tobacco plant way before the humans destruction of the plant world had occurred... "After passing these words to me I cannot believe or understand how you can still smoke, what's up with that man?" He looked me in the eye and replied in masterful poetic form.

"I've never been best of people;
I've not always done it right
I've disappointed those who loved me;
I've darkened my shining lights
I'm getting old and I'll soon be gone,
it's why I show my wrongs
My health it fades my wealth did trade,
though the story must go on.

Let me be your lighthouse and learn from my mistakes
Let me be your lighthouse, this ain't the road to take.

I've been selfish from time to time,
taken and not returned
I've stole to feed my habits,
still I have never learned
Treat me as untouchable,
avoid me at all costs
That will be my saving grace,
if not then all is lost.

Let me be your lighthouse and learn from my mistakes
Let me be your lighthouse, this ain't the road to take.

I could give you some reasons why,
could try to make it up
Could tire you with excuses,
on why I am so corrupt

> I did not have intentions,
> to create and cause the pain
> Please learn from my sacrifice,
> don't let it be in vain.
>
> I accept the circles of this life, I
> ike to know what's killing me
> Call me a perfect teacher,
> and your lighthouse I can be."

"That was quite a poem... needs all to make a world I guess, where are you going Mr. Lighthouse?" I intrigued. "To go start a coffee and tobacco plantation, you just remember that you are what you eat, and you will be what eats you. Here, have my coffee biscuit friend, I'm already full!" Mr. Lighthouse bid his adieus and went on his way.

I looked at the biscuit, this was not the first biscuit I'd had and it would surely not be the last. I began to think of meals as continuous instead of separate, like having to constantly be painting a long bridge. I thought about having a thousand biscuits stuck together before me from a thousand different situations. It seemed a grounding meal as to be munching into earth, kind of like a worm. I thought about the biscuit eating me and being a biscuit, I didn't want to be a biscuit. I left the biscuit. I felt like adopting a more continuous liquidous diet and stopping smoking. I looked at the menu and ordered myself a bowl of fish and seaweed soup which quickly arrived. It felt like I was drinking the sea instead of eating the ground. If only I could breathe in the sea, I thought.

I looked out the window at another plane take off, "Flight three-seven-eleven will be boarding at gate eight within the hour. Would all passengers please make their way to the boarding checkpoint" The tanoy tone spoke through the buzz of the airport goings on making me aware it was my turn to be on the plane, soaring away from this airport fish bowl. I still had an hour or so and I was still fatigued from the mountain escapade. I drifted off.

I found myself amongst a great crowd of silent forms and shapes I had not before seen. It truly was a vast sea of uniqueness and difference. Beyond this sea of difference was an all surrounding darkness of deep space though there were no stars to be seen. Under my feet there was no floor, only the same dark space that was somehow supporting and suspending me and the crowd of difference in this place. This surrounding deep dark space gave me a different feeling to that which I normally felt when looking up to the sky, into the darkness of space. This dark space gave me not the feeling of endlessness and liberation; it felt more like the walls of an all-consuming, ever tightening, inescapable prison. The sea of refreshingly unique shapes and forms swayed in an unmistakable unison. I could not get into its sway or escape it. I became still. I realized there was movement in being still like how silence is a sound. Something changed.

Some distance ahead, through the sea of shapes and forms I could see a darker platform forming out of the same dark space that surrounded me and this sea of difference. I could feel myself being pulled towards it, though I remained where I was. A shadowy silhouette of human form appeared on this platform. The silhouette began to morph into different forms, expanding and contracting before settling back into human form. I could make out no features. No need for features with a presence I guessed. A voice began to sing from this shadowy silhouette.

"I was lying in my tent, the day it was spent
The rain was falling on me, singing whispers from the sea
The sound of the ocean, gives me a healing potion
Could this be a heaven, we are all meant to see.
I've got my favorite shirt on, been with me for so long
Places I have went, choosing where I slept
Come sleep in an office, I say the beach is my surface
Crawled out the sea slow, there was no time long ago.

Now the journey I have been making,
no longer got me quaking
The waves of air, they seem to care
Stranger thinking I'm in pain, offers shelter from the rain
A new game in his hand eases those demands
Don't need to learn to swim, when I'm already floating.
Being guarded while I sleep by the dogs that walk the street
Senses there returning when I feel the lighters burning
When you get those itching feet it gets so hard to sleep.

There was more than just one famous man

> Hung up by nails in his hands
> A toast to all those other souls
> that had not had their sagas told
> Say history and you think it's old
> Learn from the past it showed us so
> Buried on this land by egg timers dropping sand
> There was peace in your eye,
> when you were looking to the sky
> Some knew it yesterday though forget about today."

A loud crackling sound arose and drowned out the shadow. It was an electric sound that forced the forms and shapes to an uncomfortable movement.
The voice of the shadow broke through the static.

> "I just have to say, there surely is another way
> So worry not for come what may
> You will see I'm true this day
> Now I must go, I'm blown of course
> And return myself back to the source
> My mind must walk
> My feet must talk
> So wake up friend you're on the clock."

The electric static returned, its drone infecting my mind. A voice appeared in its piercing crackle. "Last call for flight three-seven-eleven."
Shit! My flight! I'd been dreaming. I made a beeline for the

gate.

I was stopped as I came to the last security checkpoint before the gate.

"Anything to declare sir?" asked the quite butch, most likely female, passport checking security guard. "Only my balls miss" I said cheekily. I held the three spheres I had juggled in the glacier and the last sphere I had left over from the spheres I'd made in Amsterdam out openly in my hands, and as she looked at them I gave them a cheeky little squeeze. Somewhere behind her uniform she smiled inwardly. "You're late Mr. Duecourse. You had better run along now", she said it in a way that revealed the undeniable after-hours dominatrix in her. I played the submissive key with a wink and passed on.

Chapter Eleven

Emerging out of airport world it didn't seem real. Then again how real is airport world and again, how real is reality itself? Life on paper... I had a passport with an old picture and an old name describing nothing of my true and present self. 'And the cattle were branded' said the cowboy was an expression that came to mind.

The flight voucher had got me a one way to Bombay.

I had arrived in a living steam world. The street was a busy colorful sauna of life. There were tuk tuks, motorbikes, cars, trucks, buses, cows, dogs, cats, birds, mice, water buffalo, shops, stalls and people all attempting various tasks. All the busyness of a natural world, all be it a changing world with ever flourishing changing nature. Everything is nature came as a thought, I guess it's just the nature that's not changed itself and instead been changed by someone or something else that's unnatural.

I took out my juggling clubs from my backpack. This was a new country and it was a slight tradition of mine to have a little juggle in any new place I reached. After a small juggle to some passerby's amusement, I finished up and attached the clubs to my belt.

Along the busy street under the shade of a small tree, there was an old man sitting apparently cross-legged. As I walked towards him and got closer I came to see that he had no legs at all. It felt like a throwback to the past and a throw forward to the future for some reason I could not fathom. His hair was long, grey and straggly and had dull colored bands through it. He wore three earrings in his left ear and from his chin there was the growth of a graying beard.

The old man had a sign, and sat on a mat with his head bowed. He was a palm reader. I remembered hearing before from some previous walk in life that the palms of your hands tell a story.

I walked closer until I stood in front of him; his head was still bowed so the first sight he saw of me was my feet, which bore no shoes as I had taken them off on arrival. I always liked not wearing shoes where ever possible, it's like sex without a condom in that you get all the feeling. There were a few others on the street walking bare footed, so I did not feel out of place. Were they barefooted by choice was a question I asked myself and it was a question I felt I knew the answer too. Slowly he raised his head. As he raised his head on the journey towards my face he slowed as he passed by my hands at the side of my body, then continued his gaze to my face. One of his eyes was permanently closed; the other eye was white with only a pinprick of black for a pupil. It could clearly be said he was blind, though I did not believe anyone could be all blind in that surely blindness is just another form or stage of sight. I could see that he could see things also. Just a little differently. There were no words in the conversation yet, though for sure the conversation had already begun. He invited me to sit with a movement of his hand. Wherever he sat on that mat was his home, so I treated that part of the street with the respect it was due. Respect and appreciation for other people's space can unlock many doors for all, and if sincere, can break down barriers. I sat in front of him, crossed my legs and bowed. His sign read 50 rupees for a reading, which seemed a fair price if it was truth or not. We sat opposite each other gazing through one another's look. He raised both of his hands towards me and I opened my hands to him. As my palms turned and came to face upwards, the pinprick of black in his left eye grew to become a deep dark lagoon of calm. He ran his fingertips around my palms at an unchanging pace. The fingers reached the scar left by the broken compass and I felt his fingertips warming. He brought his head to meet the scar and touched it with his forehead. It seemed to me he had seen the scar before though how could this be? Then he spoke a whisper.

"A map" he whispered. "This is a river you must go to. You must find the way".

"Where do I go?" I asked longingly. He paused, took his fingertips from my scar, and put a hand on each of my feet, "To where they don't feel lost", he said. He brought his hands back to himself and bowed his head. He had no more to pass to me so I released the juggling clubs attached to my belt and juggled a few patterns for him. The movement of his head suggested he could at least feel the energy of the movement before him. I brought out the set of juggling spheres that had got me through the glacier. I passed them to the old palm reader and to my amazement; he juggled a quick pattern I had not seen before. The special material glinted in the darkening street and began to glow. He caught them and then placed them by his side. He bowed his head once more.

I rose to my feet. I needed to find this place he spoke of. Somehow when I broke that compass in my hand, the scar had become a map. Somehow it was all connected; somehow this was all meant to be happening. Somehow most importantly, this was happening! There was a hint of purpose in the air. I had a feeling that something special was meant for me. This was an intoxicating feeling as I had went through most of my life feeling the complete opposite.

Since I had cut loose from all of the ties of my old life and started living my dreams, these connections were coming faster. I had not forgotten my old life, I was just continuing it. Possibly, like Zia had said, I was following my true wants and discovering my true needs. I could feel I was connecting to my soul and nourishing it.

I felt like I should be writing these happenings and sealing them in paper. There must be something to be learned from this that could help others. I thought of it as going to a shit night club. Out of the shit music you may find at least one track that can make the night for you. That track in the static can be worth it. Everyone has got a book in them anyway. Though what can you write about when given the freedom of which to do so? The options are as endless as a blank page... The past and an interpretation of things done, the present and what doing, or the future and what's going to be doing. When the present becomes safe it gets easier to drift between the three. I wasn't too worried about feeling safe; life on the road was teaching me to make my peace with the feeling of being unsafe. I was finding a home in traveling, in movement, in a way, living the fantasy and making it a reality where security was just an illusion.

I was coming to realize that each new place with all its people, culture and history, no matter its thoughts or ways of life, that in the present, there was no hugely great fundamental differences, only the slightest glistening of difference. Media has a lot to answer for. People are just chasing for the some space in the hope of finding a breathing space. Same same, with only a little difference. It's when you don't appreciate the difference that the problem occurs. The diversity of this world is one of the most beautiful things about it. There seems to be so many different patterns and ways of life. Who am I to judge which is the right way; Is there a right way? There are many wrong ways! I would not want to bear the cross of judgment anyway. I enjoy the little differences.

As much as you would think that every new place you reach is increasing the size of your world, it's only just making it smaller. To escape from this ever decreasing external world, that can become so claustrophobic in all its size, you find that the only place that's big enough to retreat to, or advance to, is the place that's no further away than a glance inwards.

I ask myself, would I still have gone if I had known the resulting consequences of my actions. The answer to that question, I try to show myself, is quite inconsequential.

Don't expect, just accept could well be the best advice I have listened to in a jungle of camouflaged words. I'm still alive, I accept that. I knew I must find this river as the true purpose of the smashing of the glass compass appeared now not to be an accident but more than that.... A piece of the puzzle... The next step in reaching for the unknown, which I wanted to know. Why would I want or need to know the unknown? Isn't the unknown there just so we can understand the known? Without the dark would there be light? These questions can spin in circles, It seemed I had an answerable question; How can I find this river? I looked around, there was another road, another corner in the street, there were endless amounts of souls to meet and greet and endless amounts of benches to rest my feet. This land goes on and on, I guess that's why I need to roam. I thought of all the streams and how another stream was just another endless piece of thread, was it another haven, another bed to rest my head, or another level, another path down which to tread? This sea goes on and on I guess that's why I need to roam. A wind blew as another hand to help me by. I saw another cloud in the sky, another floater in the eye; it was another haze and another kingdom for to try. This sky goes on and on, I guess that's why I need to roam.

With endless possibilities almost overwhelming me I decided to just start walking again. For now I could rely on my feet. The dark sky opened and a monsoon rain began. I had no direction and was lost though I felt comforted in being lost now and felt love grow inside me. I became happy realizing again I still had somewhere to go and I was on my way towards this mystery place. Love the journey as much as the destination! Every little part was coming together and making something, though not something big, something so small it was big or just big to me. Just walking had brought me to where I was now so I decided to continue this walk and see where it would bring me next. There seemed to be a patterned path I was on, maybe I was making this pattern. I couldn't go back now. Even going back, I would have to go forward to get there...

A large truck with a canvas tarpaulin stretched over its back parked on the street next to me began to pull off, attempting to join the intricately connected metallic river of the road machines. I noticed a space in the canvas tarpaulin where some of the buckles had come undone. The hitch hiker in me saw a chance. I launched my backpack through the space. Following my bags trajectory out of the rainy street I jumped on board quickly, grazing my foot in the movement. The pain reminded me in a gentle mortal whisper that this was real and there was something to lose. I closed over the tarpaulin, covering my tracks from the ever hunting point of notice. I knew I had got on unnoticed by the driver. No one seemed to be using the mirrors in the busy street of madness and I could hear loud Indian music blaring from the driver's radio. I had quietly digested into the environment.

The tarpaulin covering sealed, I found myself in darkness. I could make out some form of cage or tank next to me and there was an unmistakable air of a stale ocean.

In the darkness I fumbled around in my pack and pulled out the last of the juggling spheres that I had made in the now distant memory of Amsterdam. I gave it a little squeeze and smiled inwardly thinking of the airport security guard. I dug my fingers into the sphere piercing the material. The scent of the green peace plant filled my senses as it emerged from the insides of the sphere and for a slight moment, its aroma over powered the unknown lingering odor of the sea. I could feel it's comforting texture through my touch and could see a shining green picture of it in my mind. I began to roll in the darkness. This process was automatic in me now so my mind was free to wander as I performed the task. I was relieved the security at the airport had given me no trouble and my stash had remained unseen, so I sang a happy wee song to myself as I rolled.

> "Bedding down in the back of a truck
> Thinking I must be having the best of luck
> Moving so fast now I hope it lasts
> Good signs all around me once again.
>
> Got some cuts on my feet that will mend
> Said goodbye to an angel, she was my friend
> Now I'm looking for tomorrow to make amends
> Good times all around me once again.
>
> Eyes got to blink it's there right
> Happiness the hardest thing that you can fight
> Monks are not the only ones who are brought to light
> Good times all around me once again.
>
> Darkness from above goes on and on

> Arrows pointing where on a road so long
> At the moment I'm enjoying just passing on
> Good times all around me once again."

It was a simple little tune. The world seemed endless and I felt comfortable feeling small and insignificant in its splendor, like a hitch hiking plant that had grabbed onto the hair of a migrating animal.

I brought out the box of matches I had pocketed from the airport café and sparked a match. I became enlightened to my new environment..

Just accept and don't expect; I hadn't expected this and I could not accept it. I had to accept this to a point of action. My heart bled, my soul wept, my stomach sunk, my eyes drowned, my touch vanished. My touch returned to find the heat of the match and I released it as quickly as I'd found it.

Inside the back of this truck there were two small tanks. Crammed inside each tank was a river dolphin. The tanks were so small their fins were forced at unnatural angles. The little water was murky and pungent with shit. Their skin was blistered and cracked. These poor souls were living death. They made the tanks look like coffins.

I struck another match. I did not light the spliff. I dismantled it and shared its contents between the two dolphins. Although giving weed to a dolphin is by no means recommended, there was no way their situation could be made worse. I prayed that it would ease their suffering as it had mine on many an occasion. A true test for the medicinal properties of the plant!

I had to get them out of here. I had to pull them out of the world they had been forced into. I could not be the person inaction would make me. These dolphins were getting an action from the reaction.

The dark monsoon rainy night, the driver's loud music and the sound of the trucks movement bouncing along the pot holed dirt roads would be my tools. I hauled open a space in the tarpaulin large enough for the front of the tanks to fit through. The monsoon rain was beating hard and there was wet jungle foliage almost invading the truck. We appeared to be driving along a road cut out through the rainforest. The vegetation was so waterlogged, if we passed a river, the dolphins could hopefully just slide into it with the slope to their advantage. I glanced out of the hole and looked towards the driver's booth. Fortunately the side mirror was broken off. Stealth was in grasp.

The tank was designed with a slide gate at both ends so that when it was lowered into water you pulled open the gate and the dolphin could swim out.

These dolphins would have to be prized out.

I attempted to swivel the tanks around to the edge. They were too heavy with the added weight of the murky water. I slid up there gates a little and let the shit filled water drain out of their tanks slowly. I used my bare feet to sweep it overboard at the most opportune moments so as to reduce notice.

The water drained, the tanks were much more manageable. I moved them both around to the edge of the truck. I only had to wait for the point of release now.

After about half an hour or so of bouncing along the rainforest road, I caught the flashes of moonshine on water. The now had arrived! I slid open all four gates and holding onto the tanks with my hands, pushed out each dolphin with my feet. It was a grimy slimy movement.

As they stretched out free from their prison, they pulsed outwards flying down the embankment through the wet deep dark green vegetation. I heard two joyous splashes, and the squeaking clicks of their pleasure before the loud music and trundle of the truck became the baseline of sound once more.

I wished I could have made it three splashes for I found myself alone now in a place where another reaction was waiting to be found. I pulled over the tarpaulin once more and sat down in the unpredictable still.

The truck continued to bounce along through the night. It would be light soon. I'll find an exit point then, for the jungle at night can be a far more dangerous place than the back of a truck! Given what I'd just done, even this truck...

In waiting for the light I began to think about how this scene came to be. Had this been an honest man bringing food for his hungry family? Were they being rescued and taken to aide? Was it poachers? I began to doubt my actions. There had been too sinister an air for any good to be intended it had felt I thought of how the dolphins had flown out of those cramped tanks reaching for the water and the freedom it offered. They knew it was within reach. I could see where they wanted to be and it was not in the cages.

If they were to be helped then I had done that. If they were to be abused, then I'd prevented that. The driver would have to deal with their disappearance in due course. Trying to explain two missing dolphins would trouble the driver or drivers enough. I also thought about the sounds of the dolphins clicking as they had reached the water. For some reason the words 'thank you' came to the forefront of my mind in the moment of hearing them click. I found calmness in the action and relaxed my conscious. I could hear the sound of a sweet female voice singing in Hindi from the driver's radio. I closed my eyes and fell asleep to her soothing musical kiss.

Chapter Twelve

The water had turned to fire. The rains had stopped. The moist heat was now a hot dry heat. The forest had been replaced with rocks, dust and sand.

We had emerged out of the jungle routes before light had come. I guessed it had been a gradual change though in such a relatively short time, the change in landscape was dramatic! There were only sparse dispersions of green glazing the horizon. I could see for miles around. There was not much to see other than desert and vastness which really is something to see. There was a town in the distance that looked like a dried up oasis. The truck bounced towards it like tumble weed on a journey to where it belongs.

A short distance before the beginning of the town, the truck slowed to cross an old rickety bridge built over a dried out riverbed a few yards below. I used the opportunity and sprung out the back of the truck. I jumped over the side of the bridge and hid underneath it until the sound of the truck and its radio had faded. From my hiding place I saw that the town had swallowed the truck.

I jumped back up onto the bridge and began walking along the dusty road towards town. I looked across the sandy landscape. If I was looking for a river, I wasn't going to find it here. I had a bad feeling about this town. I felt like I was walking into trouble. This is the last town I told myself. I craved a peaceful life and contentment. I could feel my body and mind

tiring from the rough and tumble ways of the road with all its highs and lows, the freedom and the fear.
I came to a fork in the road and chose the road that entered the town at a different point from where the truck had entered.
Entering the town, I was surprised to find it was rather busy considering the emptiness that surrounded it. Continuing along this dust swept busy street I figured I had better find a place to wash. On my clothes was the scent of the sea due to the dolphin incident, so I decided to find a place that would deal with the need.
As I was searching for this place I noticed a group of men standing up an alley intrigued with something happening. Intrigued myself, I walked up the alleyway and saw that there was a man playing the game where you have three cups with a ball under one, and you have to guess which cup is hiding the ball after he shuffled them around the table. A voice came from one of the onlookers directed at me, "You can win 100 rupees" for which I replied "No doubt you can lose a lot more". The man laughed, "Max is the name traveler, pleased to meet you". We walked away from the game and started chatting. "I used to work in Amsterdam my friend, and now I have an incense factory here, you want to come see it and have a smoke?". I was not too keen to have a smoke with this forward speaking character as something felt wrong, though I was interested to see the workings of an incense factory so I decided to go with Max.
We jumped in an auto rickshaw and the death wish driver

hurtled us around the web-like streets. This driver tested my nerve more than once as he wove in and out of traffic narrowly missing people, cars, stalls and walls. It seemed hectic to me though I figured he had been doing this for years and knew every bump and corner like the back of his hand. Wait a minute! I noticed that the driver only had one hand! I became more amazed than worried because the guy drove like a pro. We skidded to a halt half way up a narrow street that was lined with corrugated iron walls lined with barbed wire. Every 40 meters or so up the street, there were large wooden gates.

Max passed the driver a few rupees and we jumped off. He must not have paid him enough though as the driver deliberately wheel spun, covering us both in dust before speeding off and disappearing up an alleyway. When the dust cleared Max was looking at me with a slightly angered disposition "No respect you see, think they deserve special treatment because they're cripples caught between designs. "All credit to the man!" I said in the driver's defense. Max muttered to himself "Maybe yes and maybe not, we're all trying to survive here and nobody gives me special treatment. Anyway this is my factory." I saw what he meant, though his attitude made me feel uncomfortable.

We stood before one of the large wooden gates. For a factory there was not much noise coming from within. Max pushed open the gate, which brought us into a courtyard, closing the large gate behind us. There wasn't much there bar two corrugated iron shelters and three colorfully dressed women sitting outside them crossed legged, busying away at something with their hands.

I realized the factory was not full of machines and conveyor belts. These three ladies did the job of all those. "They can roll 5000 incense sticks a day each" proudly smiled Max. The ladies rolling the incense looked up from their work without stopping and smiled, looking truly happy to see me. I smiled right back at these wondrous women. They returned their full concentration to their work. "Come on let's go inside". The different worlds of inside and out were to begin again.

The inside of the shelter was neat, simple and basic. There was a sink in the right hand corner, a desk and two chairs in the middle and a pile of stacked crates to my left. Max took a seat at the desk and beckoned me to take the other seat. He pulled open a drawer in the desk and produced a selection of small ointment bottles. "Essential oils is my other business, very good for you they are". I thought about why oils were essential for some reason. "This is jasmine oil, this is lemon oil, and this is sandal wood oil". So many types of oil. "What's this one" I asked. "Oh" smiled Max. "This is hash oil". He proceeded in rolling up the hash oil in a spliff and passed it to me, which I lit and smoked on. I smoked for a bit then attempted to peace pass it. "You finish it my friend, I can do any time". So I finished the spliff.

"So what brings you this way?" asked Max. "I'm just traveling through at the moment, I'm heading towards the coast.", "Then you got a long way to go yet", "Ain't that the truth Max". Max began sniffing the air. "No offence friend, but you stink of fish. Where you been? "I thought best not to tell Max the

truth. "Take my advice. Don't buy cheap after-shave from a man on a street corner". Max laughed.
"Your starting to come stoned now I think". He was right. Thoughts began invading reality. Who is this stranger and why is he being so kind to me? Where am I really, and what am I doing here? What does he want from me? What do I want from him? The who, where, what, why and when line of thought can be so self-destructive as they seem like simple questions to answer, though they work on so many levels, you can become lost in eternity trying to answer them. Max was staring at me. I was becoming quite unsure. I needed to find a focus. I looked again at the selection of oils. I noticed that two of the bottles were far more decorative than the others. "They look special". I queried. "They are special and very expensive." Max picked up the two special bottles. "This is the essence of the tiger and this is the essence of the river dolphin". The river dolphin! "Sorry Max, did you say river dolphin?" "Yes my friend, very good for curing many things. You seem quite interested and it's lucky that you are as I'm about to go and pick up another delivery today. Would you like to buy some? For you I'll give for special price?"

How is this possible I wondered, of all the people I could bump into, I walk right into the path of what I was trying to avoid. The gods from above, below and all other angles must be laughing at me right now.

"Sorry Max but I don't have much money at the moment". I had to get out of here.

"No worry, you give me an address and we can do business

later". He brought out a book full of names and email addresses of the people he was doing business with and gave me a pen to write in my own address.

I proceeded in writing the first name that came to mind as I hadn't told Max my name yet. 'Bob Stranger. Email address:- gettingstranger@intramailer.com'. Max looked at me with serious eyes. "Now don't you be telling anybody about those special oils. Their not exactly legal if you get my meaning". "It's all good Max, like you say; no worries. I look forward to doing business with you." We shook hands. Having got my supposed details Max appeared quite satisfied. He looked at his watch. "I have to go now and pick up a delivery; can I give you a lift somewhere?" "Near the bus station would be great" I replied. "No problem Mr. Stranger", smiled Max semi-sinisterly, revealing a gold tooth on his left upper molar. Did he know I was lying I wondered. We got up and went outside. The smiling incense stick rolling machines were still busying away in the courtyard. Max popped into the smaller shelter and reappeared with an old Enfield motorbike. I opened the large wooden gate and he pushed the bike out to the alleyway. Closing the gate, I jumped on the back. He stamped down on the kick start and the Enfield coughed into life. We dodged through the compact, cramped back streets with Max tooting his horn and shouting 'Hello beautiful' at anything young and female we passed along the way. We slowed down to a stop. He pointed out a direction "The bus station is a few blocks that way Bob, good luck and I'll hear from you soon". I dismounted from the Enfield and turned to face Max. "Thanks Max. Good luck with your delivery." With that he sped off, leaving me on another dusty street like all the others.

I was glad that was over though it felt far from over. Max would soon discover the empty truck. It wouldn't be hard for him to work out that the random guy smelling of fish had something to do with it. I began walking in the opposite direction of the bus station. It would be the first place he'd go. I couldn't afford a bus anyway.

The earlier smoke still held me. I felt like I was sticking out like a sore thumb as I walked through the busy back streets. It appeared like I was the only traveler in this dusty market town. Ducking and weaving through stalls and people combined with the heat and my rate of walking, I was sweating buckets. After a fifteen minute march I had to stop and rest.

I settled myself next to a wall that had no stalls or people hanging around it. Because of the space it was an ideal place for a juggle. I figured I could maybe make enough money so that I could try to sneak out of town on a bus later on. I got my clubs out as it was the only juggling paraphernalia I had left. I looked around. Up the street there were children working at the stalls selling banana's and next to them an old lady was sitting surrounded in shabby woven baskets. Down the street a man was walking along selling tea from a steel tank on his back and there was an old man with an eye patch, one leg and a crutch walking my way begging from the people that he passed by. I reattached the clubs to my belt and sat down on the street leaning dejectedly against the wall. I was not going to make anything here.

The beggar approached the beggar...
He held his stomach and looked at me with saddened eyes. He brought his hand to his mouth motioning his need for food and then held his hand out to me. I had to look at the ground for I had nothing to give in this moment, not even a biscuit. Even given my own povered situation, I still felt guilty that I could not help him. The beggar spat on me in disgust at my apparent lack of generosity. I did not react, I kept my eyes to the ground and he walked away.

I'd been sitting at the side of the street for a while now, though couldn't help thinking everyone was looking at me as they walked on by. I guessed it was because I was a foreigner to them and looked a little different. It was an interesting experience although it was not helping my paranoia, given my situation. I needed something to happen to pick me up. I began to think of a little tune that I used to sing at the side of the street whilst hitch hiking in the past. I believed that when I sang it, a car would stop soon afterwards like some sort of rain dance. I was not next to a road but decided to sing it under my breath anyway.

> "I put my hand out at the side of the road
> Though they were passing by me when I was so cold
> They checked to see if I was a hazard to their health
> They wonder why to risk it just to help somebody else
> So they passed me by, so they passed me by,
> maybe tomorrow they'll try
> There was blood on my feet and my hair was a mess

I was so close to them they still ignored my distress
As they looked me up and down their faces came to frown
Cause they saw a guy from a different part of town
So they passed me by, so they passed me by,
maybe tomorrow they'll try
There was no light and there was no sound
I began to sink into the ground
Another layer was being built on top of me
Because they saw the difference and not the similarity
So they passed me by, so they passed me by,
maybe tomorrow they'll try
Then a passing light began to slow
A spark of hope became a fire to grow
You came out of your light to my dark you did embark
You held your hand out to me and took me
onboard of your ark.
You didn't pass me by; you saw the same in your eye
Today's tomorrow you tried"

I looked up from where I sat. A man stood next to me. It appeared my car had arrived.
"That's where all the men piss", said the man and then went on his way. Damn it! No wonder everyone was looking at me. I moved to another part of the street and sat down again first making sure it wasn't another walk by toilet. I decided I would just sit here and wait for something to happen. It did not take long.
There was a heavy set man who appeared to be searching

for something walking along the street. On noticing me, he seemed to calm his search and took up a casual position across the street. I wasn't alarmed as I had begun to notice a few times since I'd landed in India, that people were interested to see what this foreigner with juggling clubs was up to.

Another man was watching me as he walked along the street, he walked past not breaking his gaze at me, then because he was too concerned looking at me sitting minding my own business and not his own direction, he walked straight into a tree. He embarrassedly scuttled off. The heavy set man, who had been standing somewhat casually across the street watching me came over and spoke "You could make a cartoon about that". He spoke good English and he was right, it was a rather funny scene. "You certainly could" I said back. "Can I take you for a coffee?" asked the man. He had darkness around his eyes that could only have been formed from witnessing too many hard scenes. He was clearly hiding his true intentions.

The ability to judge a character correctly is a key to surviving on the road and in life itself. Don't judge a book from its cover goes without saying... On the road judgment is natural animal, not reason. This whole town was feeling wrong though, so I rose to my feet and walked along the street with him. "I'm a doctor here my friend. I work at the nearby hospital and at the moment I have some foreign students working for me, you should come and meet them..." I was surprised by this as he didn't seem like a doctor at all. "That sounds interesting" I replied. "Also, I'm the head of a mental institution here. I'm a very important person in this town you see, I have many connections". Again, I felt it difficult to believe what he was telling me so felt it best to play along with the conversation. "That must be a difficult job my friend", "Quite" He replied quickly and abruptly. "So what do you think of the drugs in India?" Coming from a supposed doctor, this question from the blue threw me. The atmosphere changed. The chat moved into a realm that was different, though why was it different? Cops do drugs; politicians do drugs, rich and poor alike. The problem comes when individuals or groups of people go on a power trip and persecute you for your own personal free choice. I've known many people on so many 'legal' prescriptions, that when they shit they could be a pill dispenser. Coffee's a drug, tobacco is a drug, alcohol is a drug. As long as the government can tax it then its ok right? A nation of legal abusers. We all self-medicate and we have to, everybody is slightly different and we as individuals need to choose what feels right personally and try to make our most learned guess on what that is. Food, heat, love, shelter, we try to give ourselves what we need in the correct quantities. Of course, too much of one thing is rarely good for you. We are at many times architects and engineers of our own make up, where freedom of choice is essential. Certainly if a drug is not natural how could it truly be good for you in the long run? Then again was not everything natural? Good drugs, bad drugs. Good food, bad food. Good people, bad people. Make your choices!

My mind was still drifting due to the smoke with Max; the hash oil had been potent. Maybe I was reading too much into this, drugs would be an important part of a doctor's job and would be common place in their conversations. I thought it best to play the ignorant card, "I wouldn't know my friend". I kept my eyes looking casually forward as I felt the man's scrutinizing stare at my side. "Hmm" Was the somewhat unsatisfied sound that came from him.

Our walk continued for another ten minutes in relative silence. The man took me down many streets and as the dust and haze of our walk stilled, we found ourselves before a closed incense shop. Not bloody incense again I thought to myself. "This is my shop where I work" said the man. Where he worked? What the hell was going on here! I thought he said he was a doctor... He must be delusional, or was it me that was having delusions? Had I been listening to this guy talk or had I made the conversation up in my head? Were we not going for a coffee? How high was I? "Where's this coffee?" I asked. "Shanti shanti my friend, it's just round the corner" He replied. I should have left then though I didn't. Against my instinct again, I decided to continue giving him the benefit of the ever increasing doubt.

We then continued along the street round the corner finally finding ourselves walking into a small place that thankfully passed coffee for money. I was somewhat relieved. On entering the quiet coffee shop, the man continued towards a doorway at the back which was screened with rags. I followed him through.

The room beyond the rags was larger than the first room and had a TV screening cricket in the top right corner of the ceiling. There was a large ceiling fan spinning slowly, fighting a losing battle against the heat and another door which must have led out the back. There were three curtained booths to the left of the room and three rough looking men sat around a table watching the cricket, eating spiced rice and roti and drinking bottles of kingfisher beer. One of the men sitting at the table was alarmingly huge. The man I was with walked into a booth and I followed. The man drew the curtain behind us as he sat down at the small table in the booth. I sat down opposite him.

His whole demeanor changed. He pulled out a police badge and sat it on the table before me, looking at me sternly in the eye. "My name is Inspector Prakash and I think you need to tell me what you have been up to?" I couldn't understand what the hell was going on, at least I knew for sure now he wasn't a doctor. I thought it best to continue to play along for the time being. "I don't know what you mean" I replied calmly. "Do you know what the penalty for drug smuggling is in India?" He continued. "I'm not sure what you're getting at Inspector" I responded. The curtain flew open startling me slightly. The huge man from the cricket watching table stood before us holding two cups of coffee. His eyes were red with bloodshot and full of bad intent. He placed them on our table and left re-closing the curtain behind him. The whole set inside this little booth was reminiscent of a police interview room, though this man was certainly not a cop and this was not a police interview room. This was a fuck! I had heard of these set ups before. I had to get out of here.

"Wait here in the booth," He told me "We need to have a serious chat my friend!" He got up and left the booth, closing the curtain behind him. I heard the back door open. To stay and chat was the last thing I wanted! As soon as I heard the back door close, I got up to make my exit. I pulled open the booth curtain to be faced by the cold stare of red eye and the other rough looking men which stopped me in my tracks. Red eye shook his head. The back door opened and Prakash emerged.

"Where do you think you're going he said. "I love the cricket, can we watch the game". I replied innocently. "Sit down!" He barked angrily. I sat at the new table in view of the cricket and he sat with his back to the cricket focusing on me. The unshaven red eyed brute that was at the table to Prakash's back got up and brought our coffee's over from the booth, eye balling me as he placed the coffee before me. I gulped the coffee quickly as I just wanted to get the hell out of here. I burned my tongue and the heat soared down my gullet though I never flinched or lost control of my actions. I had to hold an air of confidence and control. These con artists must be after money I thought. Suddenly, a piece of material flew from the direction of the table over the shoulder of Prakash, hitting me directly in the face. Prakash spun around and spoke in Hindi in fast harsh words to the men. I looked at the material that had landed on the table before me.

My heart skipped when I saw it was from the juggling sphere that I'd shared with the dolphins.

Don't drop your fucking litter! I'd practiced this way of life all my life and now of all god dam times I mess up. They had my number from the start. Was this karma coming for me?

I stood up to leave and the large coffee making red eyed brute from the material throwing table sprung up and came to face me. I put out my hand in a handshake and he clamped it with his own. "No hard feelings" I said. His bloodshot eyes were burning with rage. He gritted his teeth and began to fly a punch in my direction. He was clumsy though and I managed to evade its impact as I pushed him back a few yards, sending him stumbling towards his table of friends, who promptly came to action with one of them grabbing a bottle and another pulling out a dirty switch blade from his dressings. Prakash joined the ranks of this pack of wolves.

"Enough of this act", fiercely growled Prakash as he fully emerged from his sheep clothing exposing the preying wolf "Did you think you could steal from Prakash! You know how much those mangy dolphins were worth! I own this town and now I own you!"

I pressed the quick release button on my backpack dropping it to the floor and took the juggling clubs from my belt to hand and began juggling.

This display raised only howls and dominating sneers from these wolves. "Kill this fool" ordered Prakash to his minions.

The knife-bearing wolf came first gathering up a lunge towards me, and was the first to learn the lesson of underestimation. I sent out a club in a venomous spit from the juggle which crashed into his temple knocking him clean cold as he crashed through chairs and tables sending hot food over his counterparts which boiled their anger. Red eye grabbed a bottle launching it towards me though I managed to deflect it to the side with my clubs, and it smashed against the wall behind me. Red eye charged, closely followed by the other man, bottle in hand. I forward rolled under red eyes lunge sweeping his legs from him with a crunch of the clubs, shattering his shins. The roll had brought me under the feet of the following man, who raised the bottle in his hand to bring it down on me. I launched a club upwards smashing the bottle in his hand sending a razor sharp shattering of glass into his widened eyes. He fell to the floor screaming in pain.

I rose to my feet spinning the last club in my hand and faced Prakash, now the only other standing. He was far from the confident beast he was only moments before, standing alone amongst the wailings of his broken entourage. He glanced at the dirty blade that had landed on a nearby table and began to shuffle towards it.

"This is finished" I said, as he reached the blade. "You don't need to do this Prakash; I just want to get out of here". The words went unheard as he desperately grabbed up the knife launching it towards me. I threw my last club in reply colliding midair with the knife sending it spiraling back towards Prakash, embedding itself in his forehead killing him instantly. His body flopped to the ground.

I was in deep now and had to disappear. I collected my backpack and gathered my clubs attaching them to my belt. I picked up the police badge and grabbed the dead Prakash's wallet then ran out of the room through the back door.

To my surprise, Max was sitting on his bike smoking a cigarette. Next to him was the truck with the two empty tanks in it. Max turned around and caught sight of me. His expression was that of seeing a ghost and before he could speak a word, I grabbed him of his bike throwing him to the dust in no divine movement. Saddling the motorbike I sped off not looking back.

Chapter Thirteen

The road was dry, cracked and sand covered where the bike had run out of fuel. I pulled it over next to a sun burnt tree that had fruits that I had never seen before, hanging in bunches on it. They were a deep shade of red and like the road covered in dust. My instincts were telling me not to pick so I decided best not to eat them even though I was feeling the hunger. I noticed the partially feathered remains of some form of bird lying next to the tree. I knelt down and looking at it closely I seen some undigested seeds lying where its stomach must have been. They were beginning to sprout. I was reminded of the man who told me the story of the tobacco plant. I lit a cigarette and noted I had seven left.

I went to sit on a rock under the shade of this tree. A lizard that had been having its afternoon meal of sunshine bolted of a nearby rock as I took my seat and disappeared out of sight. The sky was clear blue merging into a deeper darker blue as the atmosphere faded into space. The road followed the natural meander of this desert valley and there were desert mountains lining the very distant horizons. What a heaven compared to the bad scene I had just been through.

There was no traffic on the road. When I thought about it, I realized it had been a fair distance since I had seen any traffic at all. The sun was hot and dehydrating so I gulped some water that seemed as hot as the sun itself, though it satisfied my thirst and convinced me I needed no more.

I heard a noise. At first I thought it to be the water grinding down my dry throat, then the sun hit an object in the distance coming towards me, reflecting an acute bright light back to my eye. Had it not been for the metallic shine, I would have presumed it to be a large stampeding hoofed animal due to the dust that was being unsettled and kicked up as it tore through the deserted, desert road. The mass of dust and metal approached me and the rock I was sitting on, coming from the direction I was trying to head towards. I had a little time before it would reach me so I quickly changed into the one respectable shirt I had, and put on my only pair of shoes over my hardened feet, like a chameleon adjusting its camouflaging. I resented for a moment having to resort to the chameleon's ways, though the lack of wings and incapacity to fly away from potential danger were sadly limiting my choice. As the vehicle drew closer, I made out a series of official looking markers across its bonnet. It had a cracked siren on its roof top that looked not to have been in use since before water last flowed in this dried up river bed, that was now being used as a road. I began to panic, though when logic kicked in I calmed down as I realized that the police would not be an option for Prakash's criminal mob; unless they were dirty cops!

The cop car slowed to a stop around thirteen feet from where I sat on the rock, smoking my cigarette. The number thirteen was not unlucky to me. It just meant I'd have to make my own luck here. There were two mustached men in tanned police uniforms sitting in the mechanical beast and before they made the motions of ejecting themselves from its lifeless insides they murmured a short conversation between them and at the end of this murmur came a look. This look woke me from my gaze of wonder as my sweat dammed and the smoke rising of my cigarette became an extension of my apprehension as the smoke blew in an opposite direction to that of the mechanical beast with these two carcasses in its gut.

The look they had just shared was the same look a pair of hungry scavengers would give each other after discovering the scent of an easy meal in the air. It was not difficult for me to understand that it was my scent that resembled that of a wounded animal.

The pair eased themselves out of their unburdened beast, put on their hats as to put a cherry on top of an untidy trifle, and started to my destination on the rock by the forbidden fruits. I stood up to face them.

"Speaking English?" asked the slightly broader of the two in a heavy Indian accent. "A little" I said, though I revealed nothing more. I thought best to return the favor "Do you?" I continued. The broader of the two replied "We speak a little". The attention of the broader man focused on the bike. "Is this your bike?" he enquired. They were not aware it was useless yet. The conversation was becoming a game of chess; any wrong words could result in checkmate. The only advantage I had was that they were not aware of the game I was playing.

"It's a friend's" I replied.

That look came once more. There was dried saliva at the side of the broader man's mouth and as he continued his show, it cracked and fell to the ground on top of the ash from my cigarette starting another layer of dust.

"This bike has been reported as stolen, did you steal it my friend?" I did not flinch at this aggressive move and kept my replies short and indirect "No, I have borrowed it from a friend" I repeated. The slighter man spoke out for the first time and eagerly jumped into the game,

"You in big trouble friend", the broader of the two gave a cutting glance to his companion as if the slighter man had pushed past him in the dinner queue. This glance made the slighter man remember his place in their pre-set pecking order, and his words were quieted to a recessive purr. The broader then stated "This bike is stolen, and you that has stolen it". Max wouldn't have went to the cops, and from the look at the beginning, I could see that from the start they would not be interested in any protests of innocence as you can't condemn or free someone of a crime that has been invented. This was a completely new incident and they were the judge, jury, accuser and executioner on this desert road. Taking this into account, I replied simply

"So what now?" Both the men smiled sinisterly now as their ploy appeared to be going to plan, I was about to become another dark stain on their teeth. This small victory of words and movement gave the slighter of the two an injected power trip and he jumped in once more.

"Baksheesh or jail my friend". There was no cutting look from the broader man this time for he was looking at me, waiting for my reaction. I was in check and we all knew it. I put my hand in my pocket and fumbled around. They were watching my immersed hand struggle like a dying animal in its last gasping movements for air. Stillness in the pocket came as the hand breathed its last. Their eyes widened in anticipation. It remained still. Their eyes drew away from the pocket back to my face, which now wore a confident disposition. Confusion rang out among their ranks. Movement in the pocket brought them back to the before breathless struggle where they realized there was a dangerous wounded animal emerging. In my hand there was no money, there was no purse, only a shiny copper police badge. I said to the silenced men with an air of confidence and importance.

"You are in a lot of trouble my friends". Their bodies shrunk inside their tanned uniforms. This was my moment to get out. I would prevail where Prakash had failed. I had found an advantage and had to exploit this to the point of convincing.

There was a limit to the effects of spoken language in the equation. I felt a free flowing conversation of body language affirmed with a selection of firm words at the right points could do the job. In one hand I had a half-smoked cigarette. In the other the shiny copper police badge. These would be my boxing gloves. I took a slight step towards them to show there was no fear and that I had a right to encroach there territory. They retreated a slight showing me the rouse was taking effect. I thrust out the badge before the dirty coppers in the same moment as barking out, "This is an outrage!" The two different forms of force converging, unsettling them further. The broader man made an attempt to reassert his dominance. I shadowed his movement and before he could react I brought the cigarette to the point his hand was about to make causing him to alter his trajectory. In this instant of deflection, I again thrust out the badge as a counter punch. "Do you know who I am?" I yelled in rhetorical arrogance. I began to move my hands in a juggling pattern. What I was juggling was every movement the cops were making towards me and between themselves. Their finger movements, their arm movements, their facial expressions, their leg movements, the movement of their hair in the wind, the folds of their uniforms, the perspiration on their skin, the bristles of the moustaches. Every possible projectile aimed towards me I caught before it impacted and threw it into space and at every chance rammed the badge and cigarette into their very being. At the same time I preached a nonsensical barrage of words. "The history of people and mankind will not accept such futile efforts on behalf of the color green and the meanness that occurs from the disgusting pollutants that brings rats to the forefront of society".

The men were now quivering and completely lost not knowing what to do or say. They surely could not understand the quick flowing random dialect but they could understand the tone and dominance of the act. One last bombardment should do it I thought before they regain their ground. I attacked the state of their appearance now by pointing at the dirtiness of their uniforms. I made the killer high risk move of touching them. I pulled at their uniform and grabbed the broader man's chin showing my disgust at his unshaven bristles in the hope of returning their thought lines back to training school. He accepted this deceptive illusion bowing his head in respectful shame. I had them! They had become completely unsure of their sureness. I had become completely sure of my unsureness. "We sorry sir, we sorry...We did not know you're an officer". I brought my finger up which both men followed and pointed it along the road in the direction I wanted to go. "Take me to the next town immediately" I ordered. I'd turned around their game and out scammed the scammers. I slapped my wrist twice to make him aware of a set time scale then pointed to their vehicle "Let's go now you imbeciles". I began to march over to the car and the slighter of the two scrambled in front of me opening the door for me as the broader cop scurried into the driver's seat starting the motor.

Before I boarded I gave one more cutting glance at the two cops. "If you are lucky, I may choose to not to mention this to your superiors". The broader man no longer appeared broader. They both appeared slighter. I flicked the collection of ash at the end of my cigarette; it floated towards the ground and lay on top of the dried saliva, on top of the ash, starting another layer.

Chapter Fourteen

As I sat in the back of the police car, I started to wonder how I had gotten to here from where I was. I could not switch off from reality yet. I knew I couldn't drop too far into wonderment, as the job was not complete and I was still in a great deal of danger until I was away from here. I had to find the key of escape.

During the drive, the land was gradually becoming a little greener and less desert like. We had passed through some small roadside villages and I had noticed two or three families of macaque monkeys living wild and scavenging along the roadside. There had been no conversation on the journey. Thankfully, the two officers had professionally kept their eyes to the front in robotic manner, not looking back once.

We entered a town after driving for around two hours.

After ten minutes or so of town driving we pulled onto a long straight main road. To the left of the car a tall red sandstone wall bordered the roadside. To the right was a series of family run shops and stalls, which bustled with people. Further up the road I could see an archway in this great red wall. There was a police officer lazily slouched at this entrance point. It must be the police station I thought. The car slowed and took a left through the archway. I saluted to the guard, who straightened up hurriedly and returned the salute as we passed him by. My driver noticed this and straightened himself up. The car drew up to the start of a path, which led to the main building. I could see the reception area through a huge glass window. A man sat at a desk and was occupied with some paperwork.

"Wait here" I ordered.

The police station grounds were well kept. There was a series of landscaped flowerbeds and trimmed hedges surrounding the main building, which appeared to be on two levels. The building itself was old though well-kept and was not large considering the area the large red wall enclosed. There was one other building which appeared more modern than the main building and looked like it was being used as a garage. Gardens took up the rest of the space and were clearly tended with pride. The man at the reception and the guard at the arch were the only people in sight. Outside the building that seemed like a garage sat two empty, very clean police cars. Given the comparison of the car I sat in I could riskily assume these crooked cops were not from this station.

I got out of the car and made my way up the path towards the reception. There were short trees on each side of the path. I momentarily felt like a giant walking through a miniature forest. This was going to have to be short and sweet, I thought to myself.

I opened the door and walked into the reception. The cops waiting in the car could see me through the glass window. I had to keep them convinced.

"Hello, can I help you" asked the officer at the reception desk. The man had a courteous disposition and spoke clear English. "Yes, I was hoping you could". I replied in a dignified manner.

"My name is James Bond and ..." The man's expression turned to one of bemusement.

"Excuse me", I said. "Is something wrong?"

The man looked at me as if he'd just been caught stealing cookies from his mother's kitchen jar.

"No, it's just that your name is..."

"Yes, yes, yes. Like the secret agent. I know. Thank you for bringing that to light." I acted as if I had been through this situation a thousand times before.

"I'm sorry", humbled the man as he could see how this must happen all the time to me. He genuinely looked sorry to be another fool that had pointed out the obvious.

"Don't worry, as you can imagine it happens all the time. I'm used to it. Anyway."

"Yes, of course, sorry again. How can I help you Mr. Bond?"

This was almost fun to me now. I began my spiel.

"I am writer for a well renowned newspaper in my country. I am currently writing an article on the different procedures and methods of policing between our two countries. The two officers outside have been assigned to me to assist me in my report." I turned around and looked out the window towards the car, as did the receptionist. The two officers were staring back in anticipation. The man at reception nodded to them. I glared at them. They nodded back and faced forward again.

I continued, "If possible I would like to arrange an interview with the head of your station to discuss the matter further".

"If you give me one moment sir, I'll see what I can do. If you like I could ask him just now if he will see you straight away?" I momentarily thought about saying yes just for the hell of it, though felt it best not to push my luck. "I would love too, it's just that I have been traveling all day and need to get to my hotel to freshen up before I get down to business, you understand of course..." "Oh of course Mr. Bond, tomorrow then?" I smiled happily at him "Tomorrow's perfect".

The man opened a drawer to the side of him and pulled out a large red folder. He flicked through the pages expertly until he stopped at a page about half way through the folder. "The chief will be available tomorrow afternoon around 3pm if that is possible for you Mr. Bond?"

"That is absolutely ideal officer...?

"Its Parmesh Ganguly" answered the receptionist.

"Well Officer Ganguly, thank you for your assistance. Can you please write me the name of your chief and also the number of this station in case there are any complications?"

Officer Ganguly wrote the name and number and handed it to me. I looked at the number he had written and wrote a number of the same number of digits on a separate piece of paper. I also wrote Mr. Bond, The Daily Scope, and signed it. "You can contact me at this number if required". I handed him the piece of paper. "I will see you tomorrow afternoon officer Ganguly". I shook his hand, turned and walked out of the building. Walking down the pathway through the garden towards the car I again had to check my trajectory and switch characters. I got into the car.

"Take me to the bus station immediately!" The driver started the engine and pulled away from the station. This time as we passed the guard at the archway he promptly saluted. I saluted back to him as he stood to attention.

In ten minutes we were at the bus station. I had one more mission for these corrupt coppers.

"You must return to my motorcycle and bring it to the station here!

The two cops looked at me tiredly. I could see they just wanted this to be over and be allowed back to their ways. They got themselves into this situation and they knew it. They had a lesson to learn and I'd been put in the situation to teach it to them. Unless I gave it to them proper, there's no doubt we would all have to go through it again in some other form. Tomorrow had to be today; then had to be now.

"You know what to do now with the bike?" I reaffirmed. The broader of the two nodded in resignation in a hope to not worsen the situation he appeared to be in.

I gave the broader man the keys to the Enfield and picked up my belongings getting out of the car. I felt they needed a little encouragement as only I knew the confused mess that was going to occur when they brought the bike to the station with a jam of unfinished business waiting. I turned around and leaned in the window of the car.

"I'll be in touch, you will be rewarded, now go". The promise of a reward seemed to raise their spirits. The two men saluted and began to drive off. I watched them carefully as the car scuttled back in the direction in which we had come until it was out of sight.

There were three buses sitting at their specific stands and a couple more sitting empty in the ashy courtyard of the station. Given my need for urgency, I thought it best to get on the next bus possible so walked over towards the listings of destinations. The timetables were written in a language I had not learned. I decided I should just trust in my feet again and get on whichever one they brought me to. I had a choice of three so decided to get on the bus that was nearest, though as I walked towards it, the bus reversed out and pulled away. It mustn't have been that bus I joked to my self. As this bus moved away, it revealed the next bus along the line and as I gazed across into its insides my eyes met those of an ageing man looking right back out at me with a strangely familiar face. I could not place where I knew him from though a haze of significance shone in the moment. "Ah, there's my bus" I said out loud too myself, and walked over to it jumping on. There was no driver in position yet and bar the man with the familiar face, the only others on board were a woman fussing over her child. I walked on by the woman and child and took a seat behind the man. "My name is Arico, what's yours?", "Its Dipak". "Where are you going Dipak?" I asked, "I go jungle, you?", "same same Dipak, same same".

Dipaks face was truly familiar and something about him put me at peace. I relaxed into my seat.

The driver boarded and took the exchange of tickets from Dipak and the lady, and a little money from me, which came from my deceased friend Prakash's wallet.

Things had got pretty messy. I was in a country that was getting stranger by the second, I was spending a dead man's money, a gang of criminals had scores to settle with me, and now the cops would be pondering the question of the motorbike and the missing reporter.

None of these situations bothered me. What was bothering me was that I had killed a man. I wasn't a killer but I had killed a man. Maybe I deserved to be captured and caged. I could not bear to think about it. I'll deal with that later I thought and put it to the back of my mind. I was far too tired to think of such a heavy matter.

The driver started up the rickety old bus and set off for the jungle. The colors of more unseen places flashed in my eyes again as the bus bounced along the road, which seemed as if it were made more of potholes than of road itself. I took of my shoes and changed out of the respectable shirt back into my trusty road beaten t-shirt and attempted to get some sleep while I had the chance. Through my exhaustion, I fell quickly into a deep sleep.

I closed my eyes to one world and opened them to another. I was standing amongst the sea of different forms, beings and shapes again, surrounded by the same deep dark space. This living crowd heaved to and fro like waves in a stormy sea. The dark platform began to form again some way in the distance and sparks of light flashed from it. The darkened silhouette of the shadow man appeared on this platform and the sea of difference calmed. The shadow man's voice rang out over the crowd and had the pull of the moon on the oceans of earth effect as the crowd began to sway in trance like form to the shadow man's words. "Roll up, roll up, roll up...come choose a future. Hello little one, what would you like to choose?" The crowd spoke together as the voice of a child "Can we choose the present please". The shadow man began to sing.

> "It's a multi-cellular society
> There are many choices for you to be
> If you choose just one then you will see
> You're giving up the right for to be free.
>
> You make a smile and you pass it on
> Slowly slowly, it won't take so long
> In this world you'll see a right a wrong
> Try your best to mix and get along.
>
> In this world we make much sanuuk
> The only person winning is the crook
> They say my friend you come and look
> Afterwards your chat and money took.
>
> Sometimes people only seeing walking money
> Like the bee to take for granted honey
> This one way now how it work
> Try to fight and you will be so hurt.
>
> One in six, I like those odds in a chamber
> Risk your life in the eyes of a stranger
> Wasting energy to try to change her

You know she'd take that baby from the manger.

If I needed money to do things what sort of
person would I be?
Why do I need to sleep in a house when I can sleep up a tree?
Far too many dictators needing slaves for their suits
Far too many spectators branching of those roots

Try to live in kindness though it's a lonely road to take
Far too many thieves out there,
far too many bones to break.
Chain me to anchors on this dirty old land
Brainwash my movements would you try to force my hand.

No buts to experience sanuuk
I think I'll share a drink now with that crook
At yourself now you must look
A goodness in you they have never took

A goodness coming from beneath the skin
Losing it when you're looking within
An outward expression of inside
To be yourself this you should never hide.

Walkings, talkings and feelings of aware
We are hero living in an ocean of air
A little love and a little care
This paradise is now for all of us to share."

The hands from within this sea of difference raised me and I lay upon them as they held me up. All was calm as I looked above to the dark space above me. I began to shake and feel the dark space pulling me into its endless depth...

I can't tell whether I opened or closed my eyes though I found myself looking into the familiar face of Dipak.

"You were shaking Arico, I think you have bad dream. We are in the jungle now, come to my house to meet my family." Dipak was right and wrong, he was right about being in the jungle, the immense colors of green shone into me as I looked through the window of the stilled bus. He was wrong because the dream did not feel like a bad dream.

As I got up to leave the bus the mother was sleeping now and her child slept clinging to her body as a baby monkey would as its mother walked through the canopies. Different types of trees to walk through these days I thought as I thanked the driver for his work and jumped of the bus.

As I had slept, the driver must have driven the bus through the night as the morning found us deep in the rainforest. The ground was no longer made of dust, it was made of mud and its moist shoulders were a pleasure to taste for my scarred feet. The air was warm and thick with humidity. The bus swam off along the jungle road and was almost instantly consumed by the surrounding green depths; its sound soon after was replaced by the sound of the jungle.

The bus had stopped next to a row of several small simple looking shelters knocked together with some form of bamboo that had rusting corrugated iron rooftops. Exotic flowers had established themselves in the cracks of the walls and water from the last monsoon filtered down from the above canopy gently tapping out a subtle concerto on the algae covered corrugated iron. Dipak walked with familiar feet towards one of these shelters, which steamed with cooking food. Dipak spoke some local dialect to the chef and I found my universal language speaking was not far wrong as a meal of delicious steamed fish and rice arrived served on a plate sized banana leaf.

"You are welcome to my house, and to meet my family and friends Arico, my son will be picking me up shortly..." Again the warmth and kindness of strangers on the road filled me with hope and love. I had a really good feeling about Dipak so I humbly accepted. I wondered for a moment why I humbly accepted, I hardly felt great enough to be humble. I sat down with Dipak inside the shelter next to the where the food had been cooked and we enjoyed our meal in quiet contentment.

Sure enough, around ten minutes after finishing the meal an old clapped out off-road jeep pulled up outside the restaurant and the passenger door flew open to reveal a young smiling boy of no more than fourteen years of age " Namaste father, sorry I'm late", Spoke the boy.

"My son", smiled Dipak, "let's go to my home now". We jumped on board and his son introduced himself as Zorbo. We drove away from the small settlement and followed a small road even deeper into the forest. Zorbo drove fast as we bounced along this road, his feet barely able to reach the pedals of the jeep. I looked out the side window and gulped in apprehension as I saw that there was a sheer drop to the left. Treetops made a ground of green and I noticed a troop of monkeys strolling across this leafy canopy which reminded me of the dream of bouncing over the forest canopy.

"Zorbo a good driver you see" smiled Dipak. After an hour or so, the Jeep began to wind up and spiral around a hill until a clearing appeared revealing a beautiful wooden house amongst the tree's. This dwelling was the most zanical house my eyes had ever seen, its simplicity contrasting with the surrounding complexity of the jungle made it glow. As I looked around my sight revealed two more shelters of unusual shape, one was about half the size of the house and wooden and the other was much smaller and made of stone.

"House, workshop, bathroom." spoke Dipak. "Come meet family Arico, my wife good person and good cook. We celebrate tonight. My daughter has just returned from a long journey. First though, I think you should have a wash." "I think that is a good idea Dipak" "Everything you need in the bathroom Arico. See you soon".

Dipak walked up to the house and went in. I could hear a gaggle of happy commotion on his arrival. I walked over to the bathroom which was the smallest structure built with large smooth stones. Flowers grew on its rooftop making it look very beautiful. Inside was a large cauldron of water steaming over some hot embers. It was the most satisfying bath I believe I had ever had. Feeling cleansed I thought I had best go and meet the family.

As I walked through the door to this inside world I could not believe my eyes. Zia was sitting on a rocking chair peacefully sipping a cup of chai! As she looked up our eyes met. This had to the absolute mother of all coincidence! Somehow my path through all the madness had led me back to Zia!

I instantly realized that she was the place I was searching for. I no longer felt lost. Her eyes were my home; her breath was the wind that had been blowing me. I felt I existed. I felt she existed. I felt I loved her. I felt she loved me. I momentarily closed my eyes and thanked the being that had told me of this place in my dreams. I had so much to talk to her about. She had so much to talk to me about. This was eternal. "It's over Zia, we have found each other". Zia smiled, and came to me. She kissed my cheek with her soft passion pink lips and spoke a whisper. "Remember Arico, it's just the beginning".

Zia introduced me to her mother who was baking in the kitchen and she welcomed me with open arms. The inside of the house was one large room. At one end was the kitchen, in the middle was a large table that could seat around 14 people and at the other end was a little table that had two rocking chairs and a couple of wooden seats around it. Next to the little table was a bookshelf filled with a varied selection of novels, magazines and comic books. A fire crackled away in the kitchen area, which doubled as a stove. Its flames performed a dancing exhibition of silhouettes on the white walls of the room. Above the fireplace was a painting of an elephant. There was not much else in the room and it seemed that not much else was needed. Next to the kitchen was a doorway that led to a staircase, which I assumed to be the way to the bedrooms upstairs. Zia took my hand and squeezed it. "Let me show you the gardens space tripper". She looked so beautiful I would go anywhere she asked. It was intoxicating. Her dark ringlets flowed over her dainty shoulders. She wore a simple aqua green sari and wore no shoes. Her feet were petite and she had a silver toe ring that sparkled when the light of the fire touched it. Her eyes had an ambience of endlessness and I felt found being lost in them. We made our way out of the house. Zia's mother spoke to her in their natural language. "Dinner will be ready soon?" I said to Zia. "How did you know she said that?" Zia comically questioned. "Some things are just universally understood" I jested pointing at my stomach. We walked out onto the porch. It was getting a little dark. I looked at Zia. She shone so bright that everything else around her appeared dark. She was my light.

"The gardens are this way Arico, come on". The gardens were beautiful. There were rows of root vegetables, banana trees, mango trees, runner beans and a selection of other delicious looking fruit trees that I had not seen before. "We grow all our own food here. Anything we have in abundance we trade with our neighbors." "Have you always lived here?" I asked. "Not always, my great grandfather was born near here though was very poor and had to go to the city to make money. He lived a life of poverty saving every penny he could. My grandfather inherited his savings. He did not spend a penny of it living the same life of poverty as my great grandfather saving every penny he possibly could. My father inherited the life savings of his two fathers before him. It was enough to buy this piece of land. We moved from the city twenty years ago and have lived here since. When we arrived, the place was a mess and there was no house. We cleared the whole hill top with the help of a mahout and an elephant named Parawati." "The painting on the wall?" I asked. "Yes. Parawati helped us clear the whole area until it was bare. We used the wood to build this house and the workshop. She also carried the rocks to make the outhouse."

I looked around. We were surrounded in trees, flowers, orchids and bushes. Some of the trees were at least forty feet high. I was confused "You say this place was bare twenty years ago. How can it be so alive now?" Zia looked around and then looked at me. "Life grows fast in the rainforest. My father is a keen botanist and has made the re-growth of the forest his personal study. It's been a joy to watch the gradual change since childhood, being part of it and growing and changing with it.

"It seems you owe a lot to that elephant." "We do. After Parawati's work was done, my father negotiated with the mahout. In an exchange for some of the savings and a place to stay, the mahout released Parawati back to the wild. The mahout's name is Gursidapa and he has a room in the workshop, which he and his family now live in, We all work this land together." "Have you ever seen Parawati again?" "Once a year Parawati returns. She has a family of herself now. We have a huge party to celebrate her arrival. She stays for a day or so and speaks with Gursidapa. Gursidapa had been with her since she was an infant and saved her from some cruel people. They love each other like father and daughter. We have a special store of food which we save for her, her husband and her child. Her husband and child stay just outside of our grounds when they return and Parawati collects the offerings and takes it to them. They then fade into the forest becoming part of it again. They should be here in a month." Zia looked at me in a way I had never before experienced. I could feel her heart beat in my very blood stream. I could sense see she was close to tears. "What's wrong Zia?" The look in her eyes was about to bring me to tears. She spoke her fear. "Parawati will be here in a month Arico. Will u be here in a month?" I looked at Zia. Her heart was open and for the first time since I had had met her, she looked vulnerable. I opened my palms to her, they felt warm and tingled with energy. Zia opened her palms. I could see she was feeling the same sensation. We clasped hands. I looked deep into her eyes. I felt I could see her very soul.

"If this was my world, I would give it to you. If this was my world, I'll make the journey to prove. If this was my world, you'd never stumble or fall. If this was my world, I would not let you feel small. If you're feeling pain, I'll change it to love. If you're caught in a war, I'll release the dove. If you're feeling empty, I'll fill in the gap. If you feel imprisoned, I'll break you free from the trap. With all this unfinished business, I'm still drawn to you. I have to fulfill the contract, I have to follow this through. At least give me closure, I feel I deserve that. There's been so much exposure, I'm left open to attack."

A tear rolled down Zia's cheek. "I'll give you closure Arico. I love you". She had closed my door of doubt. "Zia, I love you and I don't doubt that anymore. I have never felt a truer moment in all my life through all my journeys. I ran from it after the glacier. My love for you has helped me find you again even though I did not know it was you I was looking for. My feet don't feel lost, they want to walk with you. You are the beautiful place that I will always journey to find. With you as my guiding light I will be eternally happy returning to you whether our time apart is for 5 minutes of clock time, or a millennium of lifetimes."

We both became speechless. There was no language, or words left to be spoken now. This moment felt pure and true and screamed for action. We kissed.

Chapter Fifteen

I was amongst the sea of difference again and the shadow man was there on its dark platform. It was as if the shadow man was made of the dark space between the stars and had somehow become a single being, a personification of this dark matter. Every moment it looked as if this morphing silhouette would settle and come to peace, its form changed again. I did not fear it. Its calmness in creating change was inspiring. It settled once more in humanoid form. I could hear its voice.

"Closed my eyes and I prayed for a change to arrive
Final lies is enough to bring tears to these eyes
Silence stands still thinking on you
Hope commands, still walking on through

I will settle down, just can't do that now
That don't mean I don't love you,
just some things needs must do

And I would not take her,
along this road that would break her
Said it would last for a lifetime,
that's not for the first time

So much love and so much pain
The trials and trails those stepping stones can't explain

> *Wisdom wishes for the second chance*
> *Pure existence dancing that last dance*
>
> *I will settle down, just can't do that now*
> *That don't mean I don't love you,*
> *just some things needs must do*
>
> *And I would not take her along*
> *this road that would break her*
> *Said it would last for a lifetime;*
> *That's not for the first time".*

The hands from within the sea of difference lifted me up and I faced the dark space again. I could feel its pull and I began to vibrate.

"Arico, are you all right" came Zia's voice. "You were shaking". I was right next to my love though for some reason I felt lost again. I wanted to try and explain my feelings to Zia and all that had happened though I couldn't find the words. "I need to go for a walk Zia". Zia looked at me with a truthful loving concern. "Ok my love, I'll be waiting for you when you return. Please be careful, the jungle can be as dangerous as it is beautiful" Zia's eyes beamed a smile of warm energy into my heart helping it beat and aide me into action "I won't be long, go back to sleep. I'll be there when you wake". I got out of bed, flung some clothes on, picked up my juggling clubs and started my jungle walk.

It was early sunrise and there was just enough light to be able to see where I was walking. I trusted my feet to make the right steps at points where no light got through the upper canopy. I began to ponder the reasons for feeling so lost when I was at the place I felt I was meant to be. I thought of the river and the map the blind fortune teller had spoken off. Why can't I find peace of mind I asked myself? An answer came to mind.

The answer was so painful I tried to deny it and deflect it though it would not leave me. Every other angle I tried to think off brought me back to the same point. I tried to pull it apart over and over again. It was no use. Every time I put it back together I was left on the same level. Maybe I was not meant to be there with Zia, or at least I told myself...not yet.

I even had some reasons to the answer of the question why. I hadn't found the river that the fortune teller spoke of though that reason was in the air and required me to believe that there was truth in the matter. I had another more certain reason to which I could not easily ignore... I was a killer. I could not escape this reality. I loved her too much. She deserved better than to love a killer. She was so sweet and pure and true. Life had tainted me to the point where I couldn't let myself believe I deserved the happiness someone like Zia could give me. Her love was something I had to earn; I needed to get to a place in my mind where I felt I deserved her love. Maybe I was being too hard on myself though I needed to prove I was a better man than the killer I had become.

I had not meant it. That did not matter. It was an accident. That did not matter. It was not my intention. That did not matter. It was self-defense. Was my self-worth defending? Was it worth his self? It had happened and it was due to my direct reaction. That did matter. Where can I go now that I have gone too far? To this question the only answer I had... was even further.

I looked around to see only jungle. The walked jungle pathway continued on a destination to nowhere. I had to get off the beaten track. I had to change my trajectory. I had to walk on a path that would take me away from Zia. It's for her own good I tried to show myself.

At that moment my whole body twitched. It felt like a being had ghosted past me pushing me on another pathway. I felt it was maybe the ghost of the man I had killed. I needed to apologize. I cleared a space on the jungle pathway sweeping away the fallen leaves and twigs until there was a page of dirt I could write on. If his ghost was around here then he could maybe read this. I picked up a stick and began to write on the dirt scroll.

'Pre- set message in a bottle,
ignite and jump onto the throttle
A beast of bourbon, his death is certain
Hero of sport, no winners to report
Shelter around how it swallows me
Looking out from the cave at the life that surrounds we.

Looking at the potential mistake, that someone got to take
And so the knife it has clattered,

flesh and bone look how it is shattered
Such a word to use, let the free flow cruise
Idols falling and crashing down.
Head tilt looking up from the crown
Play yourself against each other,
different souls from the same kind of mother.

And thank you for the game. No need to feel the shame
And again return to the scene of the crime
Got to face the sentence just to do the time
So bail it out, the world collapse I am in doubt
What is the rescue fee to avoid another tragedy?

Distant lands with distant treks
Cover your intelligence with sound effects
To shake it up it's so corrupt a stolen moment so abrupt
Sorry friend intention measure
In your passing I took no pleasure.'

I rammed the writing stick into the ground as if it were a flag of surrender, stood up and walked on.
Zia would be awake and wondering where I am. I was now the owner of a broken heart and wielder of the hammer that had broken another's. My life and love were worlds apart.
It was around midday, I had walked this jungle path for hours now in lost silence when my hands began to feel warm. I closed my eyes and held my hands out while I slowly rotated. When I felt where the warmth came from I opened my eyes.

Thick, impassable jungle was before me. I decided I would try to make my way through it. It would hurt to walk through this thick and thorny jungle. I needed a different form of pain to distract me from the pain I already felt.

As I walked towards this thick jungle, I looked on in disbelief as the branches parted before me!

I walked along this new path which led me to an eccentric little jungle hut. It was made of a great number of intertwined branches making it appear more like a nest and had a well knitted leafy roof giving it a cozy sentient feel. There was a small door on the hut that came up to my waist. I knocked on the door. An extraordinarily small man with long green dreadlocks opened the door. I kneeled down to eye level.

"Show me the map please", he asked. I held out my empty hands "I don't have a map" I said. "What are you talking about you strange man, it's right there". The man pointed to the scar on my wrist and then beckoned me inside. I crouched down and shuffled through the doorway.

"My names Erwol Algaevich, I live here, always have, always will. I've rarely ever left this house before." "Don't you ever want to leave....You know, see something different?" I asked. "No need, like the food to a tree I let the difference come to me." "How do you get your food then Erwol?" I asked. He looked back at me with his blue green eyes. "Mother sun feed me all I need, she rose me up, to now from seed. Hence the green tresses my friend full of stresses"

"Don't you get lonely?" I asked. He smiled quietly to himself and looked down at his feet lovingly. "I keep in touch"

Erwol wasn't wearing any shoes revealing his toes which looked more like roots. They moved almost independently of him and homely buried into the earthy floor when he stood at rest.

There was a rope dangling from the roof. Erwol pulled it and the roof swung open bathing us in the midday sunlight. "Ah lunch" Exhaled Erwol. Somehow like a plant's leaves, Erwol must have been able to photosynthesis through his hair for energy. A vegan's dream! He pulled the rope once more and the roof swung closed again.

"Anyway, you want the pain to go away don't you?". I could not understand how he knew this or what was happening though it sounded like he could help me. "You're just the man I'm looking for. I've got the blues", Erwol looked at me with a glint of mischief in his eye. "I've got something that will take all the pain away. I'm talking natural keys to happiness my friend. I have some friends you have to talk to before you can go to the river"

"You know where the river I'm searching for is Erwol?" "No, I rarely wander from here remember, just some passing answers have stuck with me". He walked over to a table that had three metal boxes sitting on it. "Choose a box Arico". I pointed at the box in the middle. "Ah, good choice". Erwol opened up the box, put his hand in and brought out a black widow spider. "Now don't freak out Arico, he's gonna inject his venom into you. All you got to do is accept it and translate the pain into a language you understand and you will hear what he's saying to you". "You're crazy Erwol". "Just trust Arico, it will be ok".

Erwol's eyes were true. I shunned the cost and decided to try. He passed the spider and placed it on my hand. A searing pain came over my body as it injected its venom into me. I could feel it destroying my insides "For fuck sake, that's killing me Erwol you bastard". "I told you Arico, don't deny the pain, accept and converse with it and you will hear its message". I began to become dizzy and tired, and could feel my eyelids becoming heavy. I concentrated on relaxing and breathing and then something changed. "Hello, my names Vessa. I am a fisherman and I fish the ocean of air using the nets I make from within. The fish I net are flies, goodbye Arico, nice to meet you". The pain was gone. "That was amazing Erwol". "Which box next Arico"? I pointed to the box on the left. Erwol went into the box and pulled out a viper snake. "Are you ready for the message Arico?" "That snakes deadly Erwol!" I protested. "Change the pain Arico, change the pain". This was crazy "Ok you crazy madman, let's do it". Erwol brought over the snake, I held out my hand and it promptly bit into me and injected its message. It was excruciating at first. My mouth went tingly. My body weakened. I felt like my soul wanted away from this pain and was trying to leave my body. I had to grip the reigns of my ship. I accepted and listened hard, the point came where the pain changed.

"Hello Arico, my name is Everon. I once knew a fruit tree that stood in a peaceful land. It was a scorching hot land and this tree stood alone in its heat. Everyday a camel would walk to this tree, eat the fruit from the tree and sit under the shade

of its branches at the hottest part of the day to protect itself
from the sun's rays. This tree offered the camel a lot, though
you have to look closer to see what the camel offered the tree.
Whilst resting, seeds from the tree became entangled in the
camel's fur. When the camel ventured off to new lands these
seeds fell and scattered. Now there are forests where before
there was only one. Nice to meet you Arico." All the pain was
gone again, leaving me with the enlightening message.

"Ok Erwol, magic box number three please", "I can't bring this
one out Arico, you must put your hand into this box". I walked
over to the box and opened the lid. I put my hand into its
murky depths to feel my hand become submerged in water. A
spark of pain became a burning fire that grew. "What the hell
was that Erwol", I gasped as the pain began to overwhelm me.
"A jellyfish" laughed Erwol. Once more I concentrated on the
pain and again accepted it to the point of change.

"Hello Arico, my names Jellgo. It was once passed to me that
the true meaning of words was more to conceal than to reveal.
I'm not sure about that though it would mean that all those
places that are too beautiful for words are the most revealing
and true places in the world. I'm not sure what I know and all
I know is that I don't need to learn to swim when I'm already
floating.

The pain was gone.

"Did you enjoy that Arico?" asked Erwol. "I am enjoying Erwol, though I feel I have to go now, I must find this river. "Why
not get a taxi" asked Erwol somewhat sincerely. I would have
laughed at what was surely a joke though knowingness in Er-

wol's eyes stopped me. I thanked Erwol for the light he had passed to me and bid my farewells. "Remember the importance of changing pain to love Arico, if you don't deal with it, it could consume you".

As I walked back along the path through the trees, the branches behind once more became intertwined. When I reached the forest path again, I turned around looking back, the pathway was gone and the jungle was again thick and un-passable.

Emerging from Erwol's den I started to think that I could go back to Zia. There would be a lot of confusion and pain to work through. After learning about the importance of changing pain to love, we could reach the other side and it would surely be worth it. For now, I had missed the sun, as the moon was chasing the sun away and the light was fading too the dark as night began to embark. I didn't realize I had been with Erwol for so long. I wanted to reach Zia and tell her about Erwol though it would be almost impossible to reach her now as darkness began to envelop the forest floor. I walked a little distance until I reached a ravine, the top of the trees that stood on its floor just reached up to the level I stood at. The roots of a great tree beside me looked comfortable to be my haven for the night so I climbed in and fell asleep within its shelter.

Chapter Sixteen

The sea of difference came with the ever changing shadow man. The crowd swayed again to the shadow mans motion of change. It settled once more to humanness form and its song came.

"Yellow sky bird, I feel your heat
I rise before you, and hear your beat
The waters cooling when the two worlds meet
You're just another animal on the run.

The stranger came and he captured me
Locked in a cage and he held the key
And then the public came to probe and see
The war of the animals let it come.

Did they know how angry we'd be?
Did they think about the consequences?
Now to show them reality
The war of the animals let it come.

They build their army's in the dead of the night
Out of sound and out of sight
Consuming begins at the break of light
The war of the animals let it come.

The passing over will flow easily
A little you is now a little we
When it's over only tranquility
The war of the animals it had come.

I try to live in natural ways you see
Though all we're making is unnaturally
Release the tools and let's return to the sea
The wars of the animals; live the run.

Yellow sky bird I feel your heat
I rise before you and hear your beat
The waters cooling when the two worlds meet
You're just another animal on the run".

The hands from within the sea of difference raised me up to face the dark space and I could feel the pull of its endlessness. I pulled my head back and looked over the sea of difference. The fin of a great shark was searing its way through the crowd towards me. I looked again at the dark space and began to vibrate. I looked again at the fin. It grew longer as the shark began to cut its way through the sea of difference, its eyes surfaced and then its mouth. Its mouth opened revealing a knifed forest of blooded teeth. I looked at the dark space and began vibrating violently. I took one more look at the shark to find it was too late. It was upon me. It jumped clear from the crowd, mouth widened as it consumed me to the darkness of its inner self.

I sprung awake. The dark had faded from the light making morning out of night. There was a pool of water lying on the huge leafs of a bush just outside of the tree roots from where I had lain to sleep. I emerged from my haven and used my hand to cup a drink of the fresh rainwater, the remaining water I threw over my face. I was still shaking a little from the dream though something else was not right. I felt uneasy and my heart felt as though it was swallowing itself. I could hear my body from inside itself.

I closed my eyes, held my hands out and began to rotate. There was no warmth this time; instead I felt the breath of a chilling cold. I opened my eyes.

I faced the direction of a wall of forest. I peered into this wall and caught the shine of two emerald green eyes looking right back at me. I took my clubs to hand and began to juggle.

The tiger burst from its camouflage and pounded towards me. I off centered the juggle and the great colored beast pounced into the juggled distraction like a bull charging through a matador's cloak. It spun around and had one of the solid wooden clubs in its saliva dripping mouth, which it snapped in its jaws as if it were kindling. The broken pieces of saliva covered club fell to the ground.

My back was to the ravine and the tiger between me and the great tree roots, which might give me some protection and a chance. I struck into a swan like defensive pose with a club in each hand as the tiger crouched yards before me. It barked a terrifying goodbye, displaying it's perfectly formed operating scalpels as it coiled and unleashed a barrage of clawed swipes.

I spun the clubs at a tremendous rate matching and deflecting each clawed fist of fury. It pulled back and I almost fell victim to the ravine as the ground I stood upon came away and dropped through the canopy to the level below. The beast circled and recoiled. This was it! The striped clawed pure natural weapon of mass destruction sprung out in a great leap. It burst through my defense and I felt its grip, though it had greatly miss-judged its leap and its motion sent us both over the edge of the ravine, spiraling crashing through the branches of the canopy into the swallowing depths below.

Chapter Seventeen

As I woke, I thought how refreshing the dozing on the fur rug beside the fireplace had been. A gentle breeze blew a constant rhythm of in and out. It was comfortable to continue lying there though my body began to call me to move and as I raised an excruciating pain detonated from my abdomen and spread through my entire body. My eyelids sprung open to find the rug was the lightly furred underbelly of the tiger where the fireplace had been the furnace to stoke inside its belly. The breeze had gone.

My head was touching the underside of the tiger's chin and my arms lay out stretched with palms facing skywards. I leaned my head backwards and as I did this, the tiger brought his chin inwards, the resulting movements bringing us eye to eye. The tiger's bright emerald eyes stared back at me, though made no aggressive gestures or attempts to consume me. The tiger exhaled a breath reminding me of the breeze from the dream. The tiger pulled his head backwards and I leaned my head forwards. My face was again pressed against its neck and the tigers chin leaned on my head. The pain from my abdomen came again so I reached down to examine the cause. A branch had speared straight through me. I followed the speared branch, which continued straight into the tiger. I reached around to its back and found the branch continued through and protruded out of the tiger's back.

I had become a piece of meat on some sort of tiger human

shish kebab.

The way the branch had bent as it speared us made it impossible to slide off and it was too thick to break. We were two worms caught on a hook. I outstretched my arms as all hope began to fade. I felt the tiger lick my wrist with the scar with its huge rough tongue. I dropped my head backwards and the tiger pulled its chin in, bringing us eye to eye again. His eyes gave of a glow of calmness as we began to each understand we would need each other, as our movements directly affected the other. The Tiger appeared to wink so in the hope that he was truly communicating with me I winked back then brought my chin forward as the tiger pulled its head back, until again my face rested against its neck and its chin rested on my head. I brought my arms around the Tiger to find its size was so large I could not connect or even touch my fingertips, so I grabbed a firm hold of the fur around each of its shoulders. I swung my legs around onto its back, and was just able to lock my ankles. I now clung to the underside of the tiger's belly like an infant monkey to its mother. The tiger rose to its feet and began to walk.

The pain from the skewer that locked us together was unbearable and it shouted louder with every step the tiger took. This was a pain I was sharing with the tiger and was the common ground of understanding we had and for sure the only reason I was still alive. I concentrated on my breathing and concentrated on the pain. I was a burden to this tiger and if it did not have the strength to move on to find a cure to our predicament we would both surely perish. I felt the pain changing to love and admiration as the tiger struggled through the undergrowth. I concentrated on these new messages that came from the situation and the pain subsided.

As we moved through the undergrowth a familiar smell came to my nose. I noticed the plants we passed through were of a soothing antiseptic nature so I reached out and ripped of a handful of these plant leaves. I crushed the leaves in my hand and applied their juices to the underbelly wound of myself and the tiger. The beast did not stop moving though acknowledged the aide by letting out an approval sigh of relief. I gathered two more handfuls of the herb and applied them before we had passed their growing zone.

We had been moving most of the day without stopping when our motion ceased. The tiger began gulping and I could hear water running down its throat. It had found a collection of water held on the bowl like leaves of a small bush. Hearing this satisfying sound made me realize that my throat was dry and burning reminding me of my thirst I craved to quench. I dropped my head backwards and the tiger pulled in its chin until we were eye to eye. It began to open its mouth and I thought for a moment that it was about to take a bite of my face until the water it had stored in its cheeks poured out. I opened my mouth like a penguin accepting a regurgitated meal from its parent and drunk the offering which revitalized my whole system. I drew my face back towards the tiger's neck and it pulled back his head, again resting its chin on the top of my head bringing us back into position. I patted the tiger three times and tightly clung once more to its great form, as it continued its motion.

We had been moving for an unknown amount of time and I was becoming exhausted. The music of the living jungle was sweetly singing to my ear. Screeches from the monkeys, chirps and tweets from the birds, branches falling through the canopy and the collective hum from a thousand different insects played together with the precision of a synchronized living orchestra. In listening to this zanical music I could almost forget my situation and if this was to be the last music I'd hear, I don't think I could have chosen better.

Just in that moment of clarity that better sound arrived! It was faint at first and I thought the sound to be the start of the rain easing through the forest canopy. No rain dropped by us and the sound became more definite. It was the sound of a river!

The tiger's steps became clumsier and I could feel its body shaking as we approached the watery flow. We were right upon the sound of the river now, though I could not see it as my face was pressed against the neck of the tiger. The tiger was shaking weakly and I could hear the irregular beats of its heart from the depths of its insides. The beast began to fall to the ground. As the tiger fell, the skewer that linked us twisted and snapped as its end pressed against the ground, releasing us. As I rolled free from the tiger, the pain was so intense I became overwhelmed, falling into the darkness of unconsciousness.

Chapter Eighteen

The changing shadow man was on the other level as I found myself among the sea of shapes, forms and difference once more. Many of the forms were clambering over themselves in the same frenzied river dance I had felt before when I was lost in the glacier. As if trying to reach for something that was so close to being within reach. The sea of difference began to calm and sway in unison as the shadow man began to sing.

> "Another meal in my stomach,
> another drink down my neck
> Trying to remember, trying to forget
> Put a leash on me my friend,
> drag me to your chosen end
> Now a battle in your hands,
> heartless souls blind demands
> Maybe someday, it will all settle down
> Maybe someday, the true path will be found.
>
> It's not that the old dog, he don't know a lot
> What about all of the things he forgot?
> Now that old dog, he can learn new tricks
> Only got to change up the way that he's fixed.
> Maybe someday it will all settle down
> Maybe someday the true path will be found

> Now as before, he knows as much
> A telling tale, to find his touch
> The fever has past, to try to last
> Swimming on through the eternal blast
> Maybe someday, it will all settle down
> Maybe someday, the true path will be found.
>
> Grain of sand in the wind, what a journey it is
> Just taking care of all of the biz'.
> And I'll only stop, when I'm in the ground
> Even then I'll still be traveling around
> Maybe someday, it will all settle down
> Maybe someday the true path will be found."

Everything went carnival. The sea of forms, shapes and difference were in a state unnamable. There was an air of true happiness all around unlike the trapping prison like feel of before. I could see them all, all could see me, and we could all see each other. Their hands beckoned me upwards and away from the darkness they stood upon. Their hands lifted me, and I lay calmly upon them as they helped me to face the dark space. I began to vibrate as the dark space pulled on me. I looked out over the sea of difference and wandered why they only raised me when many more could work together to raise others. I could feel the dark space being a long journey and I wondered why I alone, faced this endlessness. Were there not others who would take this journey? Were there not others who were already on this journey? Were there not others who had already made this journey?

I opened my eyes to a bigger world as I came back to consciousness next to the still body of the tiger. A man and woman stood in the river before me. They were unlike any persons I had ever seen. Their upper bodies were naked, their lower bodies submerged in the murky depths of the river that my sight could not penetrate.

I shakily stood to my feet. The branch had caused a harsh deal of pain though its stab was straight and true and had avoided any vital organs. I'll survive I thought though the wound was still bleeding; it needed to be cauterized. The tiger had not been so lucky. The branch must have hit something crucial inside his great form as he lay still and breathless. I spoke to him "I thank you my great friend for not giving up, I pray the spirits of the forest guide you safely in the afterlife and reward your bravery and courage with a never ending love and peace."

I looked back at the man and woman who had not spoken or even moved yet. They appeared perfectly camouflaged to the watery surroundings. They both had long thick sea green hair that resembled sculpted seaweed. The woman's hair draped across her breasts, keeping them artfully concealed, and through her hair her skin shimmered a mystic silvery glow. The man's hair was pushed behind his back and like the woman the ends lay under the surface of the river. His body was muscular and his skin reflected the same silvery shimmer as the woman's, mimicking the surface of the water when the light bounced of it. The man's face shined a bright calmness and was smooth and hairless. His lips were a light shade of blue and his bright blue eyes stared motionless, back at me.

The woman's face was so beautiful that the word zanical appeared in my mind. Her lips looked soft and shapely and were a slightly lighter blue than the man's. Her skin was flawless and shimmered as the light touched it. Her eyes were eternal blue lagoons of warmth and calm. She gave me a relaxed and comforting smile, which revealed a set of short sharp teeth that looked almost fish like.

She held out her arms and opened her palms. She had delicate elongated fingers almost an inch longer than the natural hand of an ordinary women. Ordinary did not seem to have any bearing here. Her mouth motioned to speak. No words came, as she appeared to blow me a kiss, the last movement of her mouth made a clicking sound. As the sound reached my ears and fell inside my head a soft sweet voice appeared, as if inside me.

"Welcome Arico, my name is Aquacia and this is Ariquax. We are people of the Mer way of life, an ancient and forgotten lineage of the human race. Do you recognize this place? ". I was speechless though managed to shake my head. Aquacia's mouth moved again and blew another kiss which ended in a slightly different clicking sound. "Take a look around", came her voice inside my mind.

I had to deal with this wound first. I gathered some dry wood and moss and built a small fire pit. I took out the box of matches from my pocket, I had one match left! Thankfully on sparking the match the dry moss immediately took light and the fire was lit...I sat down and stared into the fire. Aquacia and Ariquax remained as they were as they watched me operate. The fire was burning hot and bright; it was time...I took part of the branch that had speared me and the tiger and lay an end of it in the hottest part of the fire. Change the pain to love! I took the burning branch and pushed it into my wound...'Fuuuuuuuckiiiiiiing Heeeeellll !!!!' The sound of cold water on a hot frying pan hit my ear as the smell of burnt flesh hit my nose. I quickly took the burning branch and pushed it into the exit wound on my back...'Hoooollllyyyy shhhiiiiiit!!!!' Pain to love...Pain to love...My heart was pounding, my poor body was screaming out the question 'why?!', my breathing began to calm, the job was done.

I stood up and kicked out the fire. I looked over at Aquacia and Ariquax. There was nothing to be said in that moment.

I looked around me. Upriver a short distance was a zanical waterfall that was flowered with strange unnamable flowers. I walked along to it and climbed the rocks at the side of it until I stood on top of it looking over the edge back down the river where Aquacia and Ariquax still stood in the water. The river twisted from side to side until it disappeared into the thick surrounding forest. My hands began to feel warm so I held them out and opened my palms. I held up my wrist with the scar and as I focused on it then focused out to the river, I saw the curves of the river exactly matched the curves of the scar. "This is where I am meant to be," I whispered to myself.

As I looked along the river Ariquax dived under water. I could see his glow under the surface and watched in amazement as the glow sped upriver at a tremendous rate towards the lagoon at the bottom of the waterfall. Suddenly as the glow reached the lagoon Ariquax burst out of the water and soared skywards revealing the rest of his body.

To my shock instead of legs, the tail of a fish had replaced his lower body. The emerald green scales glimmered like a thousand tiger eyes as Ariquax somersaulted in the air before straightening out and returning to the water with an almost splash less re-entry that an Olympic gold medalist diver would be proud off. The glow under the water sped down river towards Aquacia and Ariquax resurfaced by her side.

He looked back up at me and I could see his mouth move. A click came to my ear and I heard the playful voice of Ariquax inside me. "Come on Arico, what are you waiting for?" I understood that he wanted me to jump from the top of the waterfall though he must be crazy if he thought I'd do that. It was a good ten meters down to the pool below. I did not mean it though as I had this thought I clicked with my mouth. Instantly a click returned to my ear

"Don't measure moments in metric, accept to a point of action" came the voice of Ariquax. I realized I was speaking their language, though I couldn't tell if it was straight telepathy or if the clicking sound itself was a condensed dialect. Either way, I just had to accept that I'd reached the point of understanding and move with it. I knew dolphins spoke in clicks and I'd heard before of whole villages of people in Africa that conversed in clicks and that the human race had originated in Africa and before that we are meant to have evolved from the sea.

I had read of a rare genetic human condition called Sironmelia which was known as mermaid syndrome where children were being born with their legs fused together and had fundamental changes in their internal organs. The medical world classifies this condition as a deformity, a mistake in evolution, a deviation of the line though what if it was something more? Could it be a throwback to this forgotten lineage Aquacia spoke off? Whales have a vestigial leg that is a remnant of when they were land dwelling mammals, could Sironmelia not be something vestigial in our very genes from when we were sea dwelling mammals? I began to see a connection. I clicked. "You are starting to see the truth" clicked Aquacia.

I shuffled along to the edge of the rocky platform, held my arms up to the sky, and then attempted to swan dive of the rock. I fell through the air almost in slow motion before the water sped towards me and I broke through its seal into the silence of the water underneath.

As I was under the water a new voice sang inside my mind.

"What can you do when the water; it comes for you?
What can you say; can you make the hunter go away?
What can you do when insanity; it roars for you?
What can you say can you make the voices go away?
Arks of reality navigate the stormy seas that you see

So many days now on the grind
when all I'm trying to do is find

A simple little sanctuary,
a safe house that is free
And so I take another toke,
of the breath of life that I smoke
The faraway become so near,
things are not always as they appear.
Arks of reality navigate the stormy seas that you see.

The peoples turning into trees,
their skins the bark their hairs the leaves
You better hurry up and take to foot,
before you're tied to ground uproot
You pass or fail yourself;
this cannibalism's not good for my health
There's so much force now in your voice,
I can feel it affecting choice.
Arks of reality, navigate the stormy seas that you see.

And as were sitting here just chilling,
while societies are killing
The people's minds becoming programmed,
when there found by mechanical sound
It sound so good to go to mars,
because on mars there are no cars
And if machine world touch that place,
I'm sure again they'd try to change its face.
Arks of reality navigate the stormy seas that you see.

So let's return now to the sea and live a mermaid odyssey
And when you pass on through the sea,
a bolt lightening you will be
So venture back and forth on your course
through the spectrums as egg timer sand
And be the movement of improvement,
in this shooting star land.
Arks of reality navigate the stormy seas you see."

Click.

As I surfaced Aquacia and Ariquax floated next to me. "Nice jump Arico, I'm impressed" Clicked Ariquax. "No wonder you're impressed! I'm entirely expressed", I clicked back. "Aquacia, when I was under the water I heard another voice singing a beautiful song inside my mind. Whose voice was this?" I clicked. "It was the song and voice of the sea. It calls to you Arico as it calls to us" clicked Aquacia.

"What does it mean?" I clicked. Aquacia looked at me with depth full eyes. "Time for you to leave the land Arico... Many generations ago all our people swam in the open ocean. In a phase of earth's history, in a time when the planet was warmer and there were no ice caps, the entire earth was entirely covered by an ocean of varying depths.

At shallower parts of this ocean, where light could reach the ocean floor, great underwater seaweed forests grew and flourished. This was our home and a truly zanical home it was, full of life of such splendid magnificent gravity and diversity.

The underwater seaweed forests provided us with food, and sheltered us from many of the larger ocean predators. It was the only ever true Atlantis" Click. Aquacia smiled fondly as she talked of this place.

"What happened" I clicked.

"Things rarely stay the same for long Arico. The dynamics of earth changed. Great volcanoes rose out of the oceans and ice caps formed. The bonds of the ocean were stretched, weakened and eventually broke creating exposed patches of land you now call the continents.

As the oceans retracted the people of Mer had a simple choice to make, follow the ocean as it retreated or stay and adapt to a life outside the oceans. There was a great disagreement between the people who wanted to stay within the great seaweed forests that were now becoming exposed to air and those who felt it was the Mer way to remain in the sea." Click.

A thought of the dream I'd had of floating above the canopy became relevant in my mind.

Aquacia continued. *"A separation occurred between our people. Some followed the oceans retreat and some chose a different path. Instead of leaving the underwater seaweed forests that were becoming ever more exposed to the new oceans of air, many of the Mer who had made the ocean seaweed forests their home decided to stay. They were to brave and embrace the change, adapting to the harshness of life outside the oceans.*

These under water seaweed forests were to become rainforests as the earth's dynamics changed.

Many of the Mer learned to breathe in fresh water, which now had a place to dwell between the sky and the sea and eventually; they also began to breathe in the oceans of air. This was a time when our very bodies and mind were the tools and technology. It was a time when we changed our bodies to fit the environment; not change the environment to fit our bodies.

Think of it as a level of biological space travel into new biological dimensions. Life just finding its way.

We became adapted to living in this new environment through some creative thinking, biological ingenuity and a strong will to live.

These new fresh water rain forests with their rivers, mangroves and accessibility to the deeper sea became a new home for the Mer.

The seaweed forest itself had changed and adapted. In response to the new levels of buoyancy and gravity, a new level of rigidity among its plants arose as they reached for the suns light. This gave rise to huge tree's which created a new habitat within the flourishing forests.

Many of the Mer felt these higher canopies which provided food and a new form of shelter, were a safer place to be than the river systems. They decided to make another step further away from there affinity with the sea. Again they adjusted, refined and adapted their bodies and became used to a new way of arboreal living." Click.

"Are you talking about monkeys and apes" I clicked. "As the oceans continued to withdraw, more and more land opened up. With the Mer being adventurous as they were, they came out of the rivers and down from the trees and ventured and explored as many new places as they could. Towards mountain tops, through barren lands, vast deserts, great valleys, open prairies. Many more refinements of the body were required and the human form is only one form of those refinements. We were a small part of a vast journey of life; it's current being created through the earths changing dynamics. We're all connected. From a distant past to the present now, the lineage has not been broken, only modified where the keys of change remain deep inside you.

The important thing is that the earth is again changing to a new phase. Be aware Arico that change is the only constant that exists. The icecaps are melting and the seas are going to once more cover the earth. Water wants to be with water, and the more water, the stronger the attraction. It is time for you to remember that which you have forgot, as the journey back into an ocean world is already set in motion." Click.

"This is all pretty far out Aquacia, so what now" I clicked. "We go back to the sea" she clicked. I was too deeply involved in this journey... I had to keep going. "Sounds like a great wander Aquacia, so let's go". We clicked!

"Now hold onto me tightly Arico, we are going to the coast and out to sea... Just remember to breathe every time we break from the water." Clicked Aquacia.

Aquacia held her arms out to me from her stable position floating half in half out of the water.

I swam over to her and clung to her shoulders. She submerged and we began to bolt through the water at an almost instant pace. Every time I felt like my lungs would explode, Aquacia jumped clear from the water and I got a lung full of air before we submerged again. Under the water we flew so fast that I could barely keep my eyes open. The feeling of speeding through the water was exhilarating, it was opening up an entirely new level of freedom.

Aquacia suddenly stopped underwater and rose slowly to the surface. "It would help if you swam as well Arico, it will get us to where we are going sooner. Swim like we swim, follow the form and learn the dance. You're a bit of a drag at the moment. Dance with me not against me! " Click.

I still held on to Aquacia shoulders as we sped underwater along the river, as I tried to kick my feet, the forces against my feet and legs was so much that it shaped my style into a change. I concentrated on learning the style of movement and thought about the language of can see can do. I felt a surge and our speed increased.

As we broke from the water to breathe, I glanced towards my legs and saw that my lower body had changed to that of a fish!

I let go of Aquacia's shoulders in shock flying free from her and plunged into the water. Bringing my motion to a halt just under the surface of the water, I eased upwards and brought my upper body out of the water. I looked around to find I was at the opening of the river where it met the sea. An endless beach on either side flew off into the distance. I could see some people crab walking around on the beach, feeling in the sand with their fingertips and using trained eyes to find the breathing holes of the shell fish and crabs they were seeking. I saw a crab dart along the beach and run to the water where it sped of out of reach. "There are many way in and out the sea." Clicked Ariquax.

Ariquax and Aquacia were before me.

"What's happening to me?" I clicked. Aquacia spoke to me.

"Your experiencing Instant evolution mixed with a sprinkle of bio-space travel Arico. You already have all the pieces of the puzzle within you, the building blocks of life, and the information of design. You are merely rearranging and refining what is already there. You have learned the code of can see can do, can see can be, can create can do, can create can be. What you see and choose to be, makes you what you are and free. You reach for your dreams to make them reality. Finding the keys of change and opening the doors of possibility.

It is why your feet have been feeling lost. To use your feet kept you on the land. Where you are going feet are unnecessary. The whales did the same when they went back to the oceans... Change isn't just possible, it's happening all around you!

You are now higher than any place on the land, be it a deep canyon or the peak of any mountain. You saw a portal of change and journeyed through it. The journey and your willingness to keep the journey going has shaped you. You have shaped yourself." Click.

The change has happened so fast. How can that be I wondered... I clicked without meaning to.

"Open up Arico. The keys to unlocking that answer are all around you. You have to think of time a little bit differently.

In a single lifetime a caterpillar can change into a butterfly. A frog can be completely frozen in ice and re-animate on thawing. A fish can change sex. A crab can grow new limbs. A fly can live its whole life cycle while you sleep at night. A deer can grow new antlers. A sponge can be passed through a sieve and its cells can reform. With these everyday examples around you, it's not so hard to comprehend. Click.

I pondered this for a moment.

I took a breath of air and submerged. Underwater, I listened to the sounds of the ocean. If I could see it in mind, I could be it in body. I exhaled my breath and waited a moment.

I closed my eyes. I relaxed. I breathed in...

A rush of sweet air filled my body.

I opened my eyes and looked down at my body. On both sides of my chest were now a set of gill slits. I breathed in and out a number of times. I smiled brightly. I could breathe in the sea! "Zanica!" I clicked.

"You're clicking on fast, let's go catch some fish" Clicked Ariquax.

We sped onwards further out to sea avoiding the glorious life filled corals.

I was enjoying my new gravity. I imagined that all the little animals that lived in the coral would be quite used to the shadows above passing over like clouds in the sky. Were they aware those shadows that passed overhead were other beings I wondered? Could they comprehend the scale? If that was the case, were there living beings above me that I also could not see because I too could not comprehend the scale? Surely the limitations of sight, hearing, smell, touch and taste could not be fully trusted to give me a completely true picture of the external world that surrounded me...

The water was getting deeper and the dark depths of the sea had replaced the sand reducing visibility to a couple of meters.

"At this level you will need all the movement you can find" Clicked Ariquax. To show me what he meant he put his arms by his side streamlining, and used his hands as fins to aid his steering.

A smaller fish that looked like some form of barracuda fell into Ariquax's sights. I was absorbed in the moment as I watched Ariquax almost implode then in an outward pulse he had the fish in his teeth. In two or so bites the fish was gone. Out of the blue came another almost slow motion bolt from the depths of the sea continuing this divine series of movements, as a huge shark came and took Ariquax in its jaws. In two or so bites Ariquax was gone. The shark spun off and faded into the surrounding deep dark blue beyond.

A rush of overwhelming humbleness and smallness befell me as the hierarchical food web sang its fatal song and fear began to grip me. I turned to Aquacia. She held herself proudly and bowed her head respectfully.

I could hardly believe how calm Aquacia appeared. Her calming voice came inside my mind soothing my fears of the moment almost instantaneously. "We rarely get a chance to pass away through old age in the oceans. Ariquax had a whole lifetime, as did the shark to reach now. They have both passed through a great number of interactions, some good, some bad, some consequential to them, some consequential to others. They have both had a beginning. The shark is living the middle and Ariquax is living the end which is also his new beginning for his essence is now again in the mix on a journey to fruition. All that Ariquax has learned is not lost, for the shark is now his ark." Click

That was not a boat I wanted to catch, I thought to myself. Aquacia's words seemed wise though she could not hide her obvious sadness at losing Ariquax.

Suddenly a magnificent burst of bioluminescence from the deep depths below lit up the dark. This light cast shadows across the surrounding depths. It also cast a shadow over the three other sharks that were mere meters from us.

"Bolt Arico and don't stop" Clicked Aquacia. The strange light from below faded like a firework in a dark sky, the silhouettes of the sharks began to turn to us.

I put my arms by my sides, streamlined my ship and bolted as fast as I could into the dark silent space of the ocean.

Chapter Nineteen

I don't know how long I'd been swimming for. I hadn't seen or heard from Aquacia since we bolted from the sharks. That could have been hours ago, or days. I was disoriented and deluded with time and still finding it difficult to believe what was happening to me. There was no day or night at the deep depth I swam at, only an ever constant night.

I was trying to swim to the surface, though I could make no sense of up or down or of left or right. I was weightless and swimming through this endless darkness.

My body was tired, my mind was exhausted. I found sleep the only way you find sleep in the ocean.... by drifting off.

I found myself back amongst the sea of difference. My friend the ever changing shadow man was there on the dark platform in the distance, and began to sing.

> "I've been searching, for reasons uncertain
> I know it's hurting but I need some more
> I'm walking through a deep dark forest
> I've been searching for a chorus, never heard before
> I've taken, a road that's been forsaken
> It's got me shaking but I must explore
>
> Into these wilds, I don't count the miles
> Far from the crowds, no compromise

> I'm striving, for something worth finding
> Paradise inviting me to come and stay
> I awaken, to pathways untaken
> Beyond the wave breaking is another way
> I'm praying to a god who keeps saying
> It's worth the price you're paying, so come with me
>
> Into these wilds, I don't count the miles
> Far from the crowds, no compromise
>
> I'm reaching, beyond the false teachings
> Barriers breaching and the road is clear
> As I'm moving there's a warm wind soothing
> This journeys been proving, that I hold no fear
> I'm freeing for the first time seeing
> Enlightened to the feeling paradise is near
>
> Into these wilds, don't count the miles
> Far from the crowds, no compromise"

The sound of silence came loud and wrapped itself around me. There was no movement from the sea of difference, all the unique shapes, forms and beings present were still. A haze of colors began vibrating around each form present. Electric reds, aqueous greens, soft yellows, delicate pinks and cosmic silvers. Many colors I had not known existed shone clear and strong like flowing rivers of rainbows. The vibrations of color around the forms sped up and began to collectively beat like a heart, the pulses of energy breathed life into my soul. The haze began to condense and a flash of pure energy fell over me.

The bright light of pure energy turned to a pure dark.

I was awake and back in the lonely depths of the ocean. I felt so isolated in this darkness after the zanical quantum of colors from my dream.
I had no direction, no way point, no sign posts and no highway. The abyss of darkness offered only solitude and all I could offer the abyss, was acknowledgement of what it offered. It would barely make a difference, though I closed my eyes for a moment for the sole purpose of seeing a more familiar dark.
Somehow it did make a difference, and seeing the familiar dark of my closed eyes comforted me. My waking loneliness subsided.
Suddenly, a fragment of light penetrated my closed eyelids! My eyes sprung open only to see nothing other than the same darkness off before; all around me the same darkness.
Then it came again, a small flicker of light in the far distance like a candle struggling in the wind. I swam in its direction.
As I swam closer, the flicker became more perpetual. The source of this light began to take an elongated form and whatever it was, it was big, because I was still far away from it. As I swam closer still, I could see that there was not one, though many colors emitting from this captivating source.

The creature was huge. It was some sort of cross between a giant squid and a giant bioluminescent cuttle fish. It must have been greater than twenty meters in length from the top of its head to the ends of its tentacles. It truly was a translucent ambient being of the grandest scale. It seemed to hover effortlessly before me. It had two large eyes the size of dinner tables and I gazed into them. I had to stop myself from becoming completely mesmerized as I needed my wits about me, I could easily be this creatures dinner.

The creatures form glowed with bioluminescence. Rivers and whirlpools of color shimmered and shivered busily across its body.

Within the spectrum of colors in the being, I began to see a consistent pattern that formed a link of understanding in my mind. This link manifested itself in the form of a voice in my head. This creature somehow communicated through the patterns of its bioluminescence and somehow I could understand it.

"Do not be afraid Arico Zanical," spoke the pattern.

"You have come here to realize your destiny; You are to be a space creator and need to return to the dark space."

I wondered why. Another pattern emerged within the being.

"To create peace in the cosmos and to help stop the consuming of matter".

I wondered how and a new pattern came.

"Cosmic dust, spectrums and dark space. There was a time in existence when each of even the smallest pieces of matter had space between them. The distance between each piece of matter was filled with a beautiful spectrum of light. With this spectrum between each fragment of matter there was a shared understanding between all matter, and love and energy passed freely and fairly through it.

The cosmos was a peaceful place at this time.

Then there was a change. The first collision occurred. This collision changed the pattern of the whole cosmos and set off a chain reaction. Matter began to collide, splitting and scattering new matter into unknown trajectories.

These collisions were not a bad thing, merely gentle bounces changing the pattern of the cosmos.

Then another change occurred. Instead of adjusting and searching for their new space and allowing space, which is limitless, endless and the home of infinity, the matter began consuming matter into their inner selves. This matter began to take its energy from the consumption of other matter instead off from the beauty of the spectrums between themselves.

This is the point when the cosmos became carnivorous and matter continued to consume matter. A consequence of this was the secrets of the consumed grew through the consumer creating matter of many essences. The earth is one of these matters of many essences as you are yourself Arico

In this carnivorous cosmos, a big fish small fish, consume and create theme was created.

Then something terrible occurred. By a mere matter of chance a fragment of carnivorous matter met an equal and completely same fragment of carnivorous matter. They simultaneously consumed each other. They both became consumed by similarity and ceased to exist leaving behind only similarity. This similarity is equal and the same as every fragment of matter in the cosmos. This similarity is expanding across the cosmos and whenever its reaches new matter, the matter is consumed by the similarity. If this similarity is not stopped, it will consume all matter to its singularity and the cosmos will cease to exist!"

The pattern made me think of a black hole. Can we stop it I wondered, and a new pattern emerged within the creature.

"Not we, just you can do. You were tested when the similarity reached earth and began to consume you. You broke free and were strong enough to pull away from it and journey the path of the little differences again. This brainwashing similarity has consumed many in the realms of earth already.

You can see its effect if you look closely. Instead of embracing and appreciating difference, difference has become feared by many. This fear is the quiet manipulative whisper of the similarity and it is causing wars.

By juggling you passed on the message of space creation, matter, good and bad collisions and the beauty of flowing, diverse, ever changing patterns. You must journey into the heart of this similarity and juggle. This arrow of difference into the heart of the similarity will release all that the similarity has trapped."

I wondered how I could reach the heart of similarity. The colors within the creature shimmered and glistened and a new pattern emerged.

"The cosmos is a spectrum of light, a vibration of zanical colors. When at each end of the spectrum you have been and seen, you will know how beautiful each end is and there will be no end, you will be eternally happy knowing you are on a journey to a beautiful place. All these little movements from one end of the spectrum to the other are the eternally spiraling cosmic egg timers passing cosmic dust to and fro, back and forth, here and there.

Because of the similarity, more and more pieces of this spectrum are now missing. The spectrum must be restored.

The souls of the lost matter contain vital messages that complete the spectrum and will restore its balance and beauty. It is why you must go to them now to free them so the spectrum can again be complete.

You have already been and seen the heart of the similarity where the lost souls are trapped Arico."

I began to think about the sea of difference I had seen so often now, in what I thought were my dreams. I thought about the ever-changing shadow man on the dark stage and how it's presence and words of energy and enlightenment affected the sea of unique forms, shapes and beings. I thought about the dark space that surrounded the sea of creatures and the need I felt to accept its pull. I thought about how lonely and isolated I felt in facing this journey alone. The pattern changed in the creature.

"You are with many Arico, you are not alone. Everyone has to walk a different path and the path you walk becomes your pattern in the fabric of the cosmos. You cannot force your path on someone else, and no one else should force their path on you. As you journey your path, you must be honest with yourself and with those you meet along the way. You must show and share because one little sparkle of your energy can be enough to help others continue to live their pattern.

You have many potential soul mates out there. Many are just beautifully close relationships though Zia is your true soul mate. You both decided to go on the journey through the spectrums of the cosmos at precisely the same moment. This launched you both on a synchronized trajectory.

You will always travel on a close and overlapping path to Zia if she lives her path and you live yours. You will spiral through the spectrums together eternally experiencing true love, seeing and sharing the whole spectrum between each other.

This can't happen until all of the lost souls are freed and the spectrum is once more complete. Balance will be restored leaving space and energy filled spectrums between everyone. The cosmos will cease to be carnivorous and matter will be able to survive on the pure energy passed between each other. There will be no bigger fish or hunter in the mist. No pain, hunger or death, only blissful existence. Existence in peace and an entirely connected cosmos, where love is the infinite fuel of cosmic motion."

The word zanical appeared in my mind. The creature's body began vibrating. From its great mantle to the tips of its tentacles, the whirlpools and rivers of colors were pulsating and flowing through thousands of different patterns. As I tried to read the patterns a flash of pure energy blinded me.

I felt an almighty force pulling me. I began to soar upwards through the water column towards the ocean's surface at an incredible rate. As I burst through the ocean's surface a deafening bang erupted as I transformed into a flash of lightning, sizzling skywards up through the atmosphere outwards into space. I could feel my motion hurtling through space getting faster and faster before another deafening bang echoed through my very essence. A collision had come, the motion ceased.

Chapter Twenty

I found myself back in my human form, standing on a dark platform before the sea of unique beings, shapes and forms. They were focused on nothingness... on me. Their ocean of collective energy stirred with anticipation.

The sea of difference stretched a great distance in every direction. Beyond them, a desert of darkness imprisoned them. This was the heart of the similarity!

I stood on the raised dark platform in the place of the ever changing shadow. I was the ever changing shadow! I was meant to juggle though I had nothing to juggle. I began to sing.

> "I remember the plight, I saw spectrums so bright
> And they shined in the night, a survival fight
> Though I saw the spectrums no more,
> I saw the movement no more.
>
> Demon chessboard the sight,
> horse bore weight from the knight
> To ride into the light, a survival fight
> Though I saw the spectrums no more,
> I saw the movement no more.
>
> It's a camouflaged suit, so they can eat the fruit
> On poor shoulders there boot,

> growing right from the root
> Soar through the spectrums, see more,
> and soar through the movement see more.
>
> With so much to explore, take a walk through that door
> A knock to loud to ignore, from the heart I implore
> Soar through the spectrums see more,
> soar through the movement see more."

The song caused a ripple of energy in the sea of difference. The ripple soon became a wave as it passed over every member of the crowd, as if each individual had added a little to it as it passed them in snowball effect. The wave of energy did a single revolution of the crowd before rolling away into the desert of darkness which swallowed and consumed it.
My hand began to feel warm. I held out my hand in the direction of the heat and opened my palm. A flash of light from the dark space struck my palm. I looked at the palm of my hand. I was holding a single sphere of pure energy.
I began to sing again.

> "I watched you lay without fright
> A peaceful child on fearful night.
> Your dreams so pure keep the barrier of truth
> If the barrier gone will you wake to see dawn.
> For hungry mouths will feed on thee
> Consumed to them you will be
> Their fire within is a furnace to stoke

The innocent there kindling the source of their smoke.

    So pass on your secrets I'll pass on mine to
    I love when your reply is simply true
    It is a sign that I'm reaching to you
    For we are all teachers of cosmical school.

    Another war has came such a shame
    Consequence was killed and maimed who to blame?
    The orphaned parent he lives vengeance eyes
    The orphaned child grows the same in its rise.
    In moments of power trips
    Their grip on reality slips
    Reassess needs to escape from the greed's
    A small sacrifice to plant the new seeds.

    So pass on your secrets I'll pass on mine to
    I love when your reply is simply to true
    It is a sign that I'm reaching to you
    For we are all teachers of cosmical school."

The song caused another ripple of energy amongst the sea of difference. The ripple became a wave like before and was swept away into the desert of darkness. Again my hand felt warm so I opened my palm towards the direction of heat. The flash of light came from the darkness and I caught the second sphere of pure energy.
Once more, I began to sing.

Hey mister energy stealer
Are you an energy dealer
Am I meant to be impressed?
By all of your created stress.

Hey mister paranoia
I've been sent here to destroy ya
Gonna change all of your fears
And start to cry those happy tears.

Hey mister dark space
You should know that I've got to kiss your face
It's just part of my chase
To create a breathing space

Hey mister collision man
Got to avoid you the best that I can
That sinister smile on your face
Says between us we need to make space.

Hey mister stars in the sky
I got to pass you on by
So check your trajectory
Synchronicity it is collision free.

Hey mister energy stealer
Now you're an energy dealer
And I am so impressed

By all of your created zest.

Another ripple of energy began in the sea of difference. The ripple swirled around the crowd gathering each intricate part of energy becoming a wave and swept off into the dark space. I held my hand out towards the warmth, opened my palm and the flash of light returned from the desert of darkness. This time the flash landed somewhere within the sea of difference.

I looked out across the sea of unique beings, shapes and forms and they began to part before me, creating a corridor through the crowd. A man emerged from the crowd and stood at the other end of the corridor holding the third sphere of energy.

"My apologies Arico, I didn't mean to catch this. My names Jamma, it's just old habits."

Jamma's face was full of warmth and his happiness filled me with light.

"Remember Arico; juggling can save!"

With these words and a friendly wink Jamma threw the third sphere to me. The sphere flew straight and true and I began to juggle directly from Jamma's pass.

Within the juggle the spectrum of colors and light flashed zanically. The spectrums of light from within the juggle began bursting out in laser beams, reaching each member of the sea of difference penetrating their hearts and souls, sending them into a state of euphoria. I looked around the crowd which now pulsated like the river rainbow.

Something wonderful was happening...

About half way into the sea of difference, a single being suddenly transformed into a bolt of lightning and shot off into the dark space. The knock on effects of this can only be described as purely zanical.

Each member of this sea of difference began to transform into bolts of lightning shooting off into the dark space. There were bolts of lightning of color I had never before seen, all launching off on different trajectories into the dark space. It was like the beginning of a tremendous fireworks show of epic proportion that was too impossible to scale.

This incredible event of motion, color and sound continued until only I remained.

Without the sea of difference surrounding me, I found myself floating in the dark space, the juggle the only thing I held onto. Each member of the sea of difference were not gone completely though. They had become a zanical starry cosmos all around me and I felt connected to them all!

A feeling grew inside me that I could not understand at first. I searched my heart again and the feeling would not go. I felt lost! Almost instantly I felt found in being lost as I realized where I had to be. I pulled my hands away from the juggle. The juggle continued to spin and spiral before me as I remained comfortably motionless. Many patterns flashed within its creative realms. The bee and the honey pattern came to me. The juggle sped faster and faster without collision until it became a blurry haze. I felt completely at ease. In the juggles haze, I could see a space in the patterns and a link of understanding came. I could see a zanical number of suns. The suns began imploding, inhaling like the breath of a giant space whale then bursting into a zanical number of pieces exploring and adapting in all directions without collision, sweeping calmly outward like the deep vibrative voice of an elephant. The grains of matter swept towards me. I could see a space and my dreams through the movement. I reached for them.

By Allan Jackson

ScruffyRed Publications (c) 2014